LB

10 APR 2012

SHAFTESBURY LIBRARY
Tel: 01747 852256

6. 15

- Please return items before closing time on the last date stamped to avoid charges.
- Renew books by phoning 01305 224311 or online www.dorsetforyou.com/libraries
- Items may be returned to any Dorset library.
- Please note that children's books issued on an adult card will incur overdue charges.

Dorset County Council
Library Service

DL/2372 dd05450

Higgledy
Piggledy

Higgledy Piggledy

The Ultimate Pig Miscellany

RICHARD LUTWYCHE

First published in the UK in 2010
by Quiller, an imprint of Quiller Publishing Ltd

British Library Cataloguing-in-Publication Data
A catalogue record for this book
is available from the British Library

ISBN 978 1 84689 074 1

Design and typesetting by Paul Saunders
Printed in China

Quiller

An imprint of Quiller Publishing Ltd
Wykey House, Wykey, Shrewsbury, SY4 1JA
Tel: 01939 261616 Fax: 01939 261606
E-mail: info@quillerbooks.com
Website: www.countrybooksdirect.com

Contents

Foreword

PIGS HAVE CAPTURED PEOPLE'S imagination for centuries and I, for one, find them endlessly interesting. In fact, one of the reasons I chose to farm pigs was because, of all the farm animals I had come across during my student years, pigs were the most enigmatic of them all. Much maligned creatures, I wanted to know more about them and their behaviours and over the last seven years have learnt just how intelligent and versatile these beasts are.

With this little book, Richard has captured the importance of this animal through anecdotes, quotations and facts and shows how references to pigs, swine, hogs – call them what you will – have infiltrated everyday life.

Richard has worked tirelessly with the Rare Breeds Survival Trust to promote and support our rare breed native breeds and his collection of piggy facts and trivia is an endless source of amusement and fun.

Enjoy!

JIMMY DOHERTY

Acknowledgements

The Author and Publishers are grateful to the following for permission to reproduce copyright material in this book:

Animal Farm by George Orwell (Copyright © George Orwell 1945) reprinted by permission of Bill Hamilton as the Literary Executor of the Estate of the late Sonia Bronwell Orwell and Secker & Warburg Ltd.

Sigh No More by Noel Coward, work and Methuen Drama, an imprint of A & C Black Publishers Ltd.

Extract from a letter from D H Lawrence to Aldous Huxley reprinted by kind permission of Pollinger Ltd.

Every effort has been made to trace copyright owners but in a few cases this has not been possible. The publishers will be happy to include details in future editions.

Signboard (front cover) by iStockphoto.

Modern photographs are all by the author except for those on pages 13 and 183 which are by Mrs Gabriel Dudley.

Introduction

PIGS ARE REMARKABLE ANIMALS in so many different ways. I didn't really realise this when, as a boy, I spent my childhood growing up amongst a herd of pedigree Wessex Saddlebacks on a mixed arable farm in Surrey. It was a case of not seeing the wood for the trees – they were all around me and I just took their special qualities for granted.

But as I spread my wings, albeit in a limited way, and moved away from life on the farm, so it became clear to me that pigs were among the most misunderstood of all creatures. The epithets we use – dirty, greedy, lazy, stupid, smelly and many more – are so misplaced as to be laughable. Take just one still commonly used expression – 'to sweat like a pig'. Who came up with that? Was it a farmer, surrounded by swine all day long or was it just a slick guy who was clever with words? The reason I ask is that pigs don't sweat, as such: they're like dogs, they pant and have a wet nose as a means of controlling their temperature. However, because we've developed the breeding of almost all pigs to be bigger than any dog, they need help in hot weather and like nothing better than to get into a mud bath or 'wallow'. They do this both to keep their temperature down and to provide a sun block, since they are among the few creatures that share with man the dangers of getting sunburnt. So, is the pig dirty and stupid? Or is he, indeed, very clever?

Pigs are highly intelligent. Anything a dog can do, a pig can do too. Pigs have apparently been trained to herd sheep, to point and retrieve game, and been put to harness to draw carts and implements; they have become sniffer pigs detecting drugs and been used by farmers in the States to protect turkeys from coyotes; they can find truffles, save lives and much more. Not least, they have been trained to perform complicated tricks in music hall turns and in circuses.

Furthermore, we use many parts of them in medicine, from insulin for diabetics to skin for burns victims. A whole new industry is poised to take off in the 21st century with transgenic pigs bred to provide replacement organs for transplanting into humans. You see, the pig is so much more than a pork chop or a gammon steak.

Scientists have, as is their wont, subjected various animals to intelligence tests and have ranked the animal kingdom accordingly. Thus there is man at the top with the great apes, the whales and the dolphins. Also in the top ten are elephants – the cleverest of quadrupeds – and pigs. That puts them above all other four-legged creatures, including dogs and horses – so eat your hearts out, Lassie, Rin Tin Tin and Trigger. Babe, Miss Piggy and Napoleon are all up there above you.

One test used to determine intelligence is the mirror test, in which pigs rank very highly. At the University of Cambridge in America, young pigs of between four and eight weeks old were exposed to a mirror in their pen. Initially they were cautiously curious, edging up to the mirror and nuzzling the surface. When the mirror was placed in their pen the next day, they were blasé – they'd seen it all before.

The next stage was to place the mirror in the pen together with a bowl of food that could only be seen as a reflection in the mirror. The pigs turned away and looked behind them until they found the food. In another pen, a group of pigs that had never experienced a mirror were exposed to the same experiment. They spent their time going behind the mirror in search of their meal.

But you don't need to be a scientist to appreciate the worth of pigs. Anyone with a crumb of humanity who works with swine will tell you that they are clever and affectionate. 'Dogs look up to you, cats look down on you but pigs is equal' was an aphorism coined not by a man with a PhD but by a peasant with first-hand experience of the noble hog.

And yet, the pig provides us with so much that is so good. Roast pork with crackling; the sizzling bacon rasher; a ham sandwich made with crusty white bread; that glistening brown sausage just waiting to be cut into; a delicious pork pie, the highlight of a picnic on a hot summer's day. Never was a meat producer so versatile nor so efficient as the pig – for 'you can eat all the pig bar the squeal'.

So there it is. The true all-rounder above all others: top of the averages of both batting and bowling and a demon fielder to boot.

So what is this little book all about? It is, in short, a celebration of how much the pig has influenced our lives and helped enrich them. It could never be completely comprehensive and there are of course many more examples than I have included here, but I hope that the book provides a testament to the rich vein of porcine activity that we as mankind have recognised and captured for use as our own. You will find that we are surrounded by words and images, expressions and symbols all pertaining to an animal that so many in the world treat with disdain.

So let *Higgledy Piggledy* be a little nugget of PR on behalf of the pig. A small righting of so many wrongs, for we owe the pig a great deal more than he ever owed us.

RICHARD LUTWYCHE
Cirencester, 2010

An A to Z of Slang and Cant

A brindled pig will make a good brawn to breed on a catch-phrase in 17th and 18th C. Similar to 'a red-headed man will make a good stallion'.

After you with the trough applied to someone who has just belched, implying pig-like habits in eating. 20th C.

A good voice to beg bacon a harsh or unpleasant voice. Late 17–18th C.

A hog in armour a lout in fine clothes. Mid 17th to early 20th C.
– members of the Rifle Volunteers. 19th C.
– an iron ship, naval slang. Mid 19th C.

Anthony pig the smallest of the litter, the runt. 16th to early 20th C.

A pig of one's own sow generally 'to give a pig etc' meaning to repay in kind. 16th to late 19th C.

A pig-on-bacon financial. Concerning the drawing of post-dated cheques. 20th C. Obsolete.

As clean as a pig-sty an ironic phrase describing a dirty or untidy dwelling. Anglo-Irish. Late 19–20th C.

As drunk as a sow a variation on 'David's sow', 19–20th C. Obsolete.

As drunk as David's (later Davy's) sow inebriated. See the story of Davy's sow on page 75. 'When he comes home… as drunk as David's sow, he does nothing but lie snoring all night long by my side.' Erasmus by Bailey, 1733.

As happy as a pig in shit very happy and not giving a damn. 19–20th C. The American version refers to a pig in clover.

As popular as a pork chop in a synagogue very unpopular. 20th C.

As snug as a pig in pease straw in great comfort or luxury. 17th C.

Bacon and eggs legs. Australian rhyming slang. 20th C.

Bacon bonce someone who is slow or thick. 20th C.

As snug as a pig in pease straw.

Bacon-faced round or full faced. Late 17–19th C.

Bacon-fed fat and greasy. Late 16–19th C.

Bacon-hole the mouth. RAF since 1940.

Bacon-slicer a country dweller or rustic. Mid 17th to early 19th C.

Bacon-tree a pig, because pigs 'grow' bacon. Lancashire, 19th C.

A bacon-slicer.

Bartholomew Pig A very fat person, esp. male, from the custom of serving pork from a fat roast pig at the Bartholomew Fair in London (1133–1855). 16–17th C. usage.

Big enough to choke a hog pretty big. American, 20th C.

Bleed like a pig/like a stuck pig to bleed profusely. 17–20th C.

Blind pig a speakeasy from the period of prohibition in the US. 1920s/1930s.

Blue Boar a venereal ulcer. Late 18–19th C. May be derived from the famous Blue Boar tavern in Eastcheap, London, where prostitution was rife.

Brandy is Latin for pig and goose a catch phrase excuse for drinking a tot of brandy after eating pig or goose meat, *c.* 1780–1880.

Bristol hog a man from Bristol. Late 18–19th C.

By fits and starts as the hog pisseth in a jerky fashion – intermittently. 18–19th C.

Captain Cook or Cooker New Zealand slang for feral pigs on the NZ islands believed to have been introduced by Captain Cook. Late 19th C.

Chaw-bacon a yokel. Early 19th C.

Cherry hog dog, rhyming slang. Mid 19–20th C.

China Street Pig a Bow Street runner or early policeman. 1810–1830.

Chitterlings the frills on a shirt, esp. a dress shirt, which resemble the small bowel of the pig.
– human guts. Mid 18–19th C.

Cold pig the act of pulling bedclothes off someone in order to get them up. Late 18th to late 19th C.
– goods returned from on sale. 19th C.
– a corpse. Medical slang. 19th C.
– cold calling or door-to-door selling, Australian. 20th C.

Come sailing in a sow's ear to be lucky; to prosper. 17–18th C.

Couch a hogshead to lie down to sleep. 16–19th C.

Couch a porker a variation on the above. 18th C.

Cozza a pig, pork or bacon – from the Hebrew *chazar*.

Cozzer a policeman, from the same derivation. 1930s.

Cry pork acting as an undertaker's tout. Late 18th to mid 19th C.

Cunning as a dead pig ironic term for someone who is stupid. 18th C.

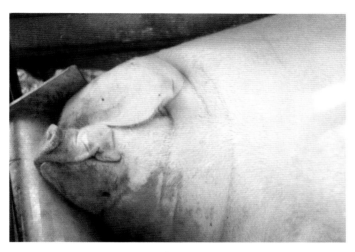

To couch a hogshead.

Dead sow's eye a tailor's expression for a badly made buttonhole. 19th C.

Dobbs obscure military expression for pork. 19–20th C. Obsolete.

Drill pig an army drill sergeant. 20th C.

Drive one's pigs/hogs to market to snore. 18–20th C. Obsolete.

Eggs and bacon HMS Agamemnon. Naval, 18th to early 19th C.

Essence of pig shit applied to an attractive girl. Naval. 20th C.

Excuse my pig, he's a friend applied to someone who has belched. 20th C.

Fine ham-an'-haddie! nonsense or rubbish. Glasgow slang. Early 20th C.

Flying Pig World War I slang for a heavy trench mortar shell.
– a flying torpedo. World War II.
– a Vickers Vulcan aeroplane from the 1920s. Named after its appearance, not implying an inability to fly.

French Pig a boil or pimple, especially one associated with venereal disease. 19–20th C. Obsolete.

Frig-pig someone who fusses about nothing. 18–19th C.

Fritter a firelighter made from bacon fat wrapped in rags. Tramp's slang, 20th C.

Fuck-pig someone who is very unpleasant. 20th C.

Gabardine swine World War II slang for staff officers in Cairo.

Gammon rubbish, nonsense. Early 19–20th C.

Gammon and patter chatter. Rhyming slang. 18–19th C.

Gammon the draper said of a man without a shirt whose coat is done up to the collar to disguise the fact. Early 19th C.

Go at it like a pig at a tater to be very enthusiastic. Late 19–20th C.

Go the complete swine quasi-refined London version of American 'go the whole hog'. Late 19th C. Obsolete.

Gourock ham a salted herring. Scottish slang. 19th C.

Grease or stuff a fat pig in the arse to give unnecessarily to the well-off; to fawn. 17–19th C. Obsolete.

Greasy pig Australian expression describing a bet laid on heads after a long run of tails, or vice versa. 20th C.

Ground-squirrel naval term for a pig. Origin unknown. 19th C.

Grunter originally any grunting animal but evolved from Middle English as a word for a pig. Mid 16–20th C.
– a suckling pig 17th C.
– a shilling from late 18th C but from 1840, a sixpence.

– a member of the constabulary, 19th C.
– tailor's slang for someone who constantly complains. Late 19th C.
– a car. Lower classes slang in 1920s.
– naval officer 20th C.

Grunter's gig a Bath Chap, a smoked cured meat made from the pig's face. 18–19th C.

Grunting cheat a pig. 16–18th C.

Grunting peck meat from the pig. 17–19th C.

Gruntling a pig. 18th C.

Half a grunter a sixpence. Late 19th C (see also Grunter, above).

Half a hog a sixpence. Late 17–19th C.

Ham actor a second-rate actor. Probably related to 'hamfatter', a 19th century derisive term for an actor based on the fact that they used ham fat before cold cream was available to remove their make-up. 19–20th C.

Ham and beef rhyming slang for a chief prison warder. 20th C.

Ham and eggs legs. Rhyming slang. From 1870 onwards.

Ham and egg shift miner's shift from 10.00–18.00 hours, from the habit of eating ham beforehand and eggs afterwards. 19–20th C.

Ham and High the *Hampstead and Highgate Express*, a weekly local newspaper. 19th C.

Ham-bags a pair of girl's knickers. Late 19th to early 20th C.

Ham-bone Hampden bomber, a World War II aircraft. Current only during the war.
– an amateur musician playing with professionals, from which 'ham actor' is likely to have derived. (Late 19th C.)
– a sextant in naval slang. 20th C.

Ham-fisted clumsy – originally RAF. 20th C.

Ham-frill girls' running shorts. 20th C.

Ham-handed naval version of ham-fisted. 20th C.

Hampshire hog a native of Hampshire. 17–20th C.

Hamshank an American: rhyming slang for 'Yank'. Late 20th C.

Hams shrunk 19th C tailors' slang for trousers shrunk at the thigh.

Have boiled pig at home. To be master in one's own home, 'an allusion to a well known poem and story', Grose, 1785: coll.: *c.* 1780–1830.

Have more sauce than pig to be rude or impertinent: cheeky. 17–18th C.

Have you pigs in your belly? The precursor to 'Excuse my pig, he's a friend' (see above). 18th C.

Hen's fruit and hog's body eggs and bacon. Naval, 20th C.

Her clothes sit on her like a saddle on a sow's back catch phrase applied to a scruffy or poorly-dressed woman. Late 17th to mid 18th C.

Herring-hog a nautical term for a porpoise. Mid 19–20th C.

High on the hog to be well to do, prosperous. US, 20th C.

High on the hog? An early American postcard.

Hinge and pluck butchers' slang referring to the heart, liver and lights of a pig. 19th C.

Hog a shilling. 17–20th C. (Sometimes also a sixpenny piece – see Grunter/ Half a grunter/Half a hog, above.)
– a student of St John's College, Cambridge. 17–19th C.
– King Richard III.
– half a crown. Late 19th C.
– a Harley Davidson motorbike, as known to Hell's Angels. 20th C.
– a locomotive. Canadian 20th C.
– a heavy drug user, a junkie. 20th C.
– a stiff brush for cleaning the underwater parts of the hull of a vessel. US, 20th C.
– in the sport of curling, a stone which fails to cross the hog score, 20th C.

Hog age that period in adolescence between childhood and manhood. US, 20th C.

Hog and hominy pork and cornbread, but used to describe any simple but nourishing rations. US, 20th C.

Hog and panther to cajole or henpeck someone. US, 20th C.

Hogback geological term for a ridge with sloping sides and a crest, the outline of which looks like a pig's body. (US)

Hog Butcher to the World nickname for Chicago after it became the centre of the American pork processing industry in the latter part of the 19th century.

Hog-caller a scream. 20th C.
– a loud person, 20th C.

Hog-fat a good-for-nothing person. Australian, 20th C.

Hogger someone who raises pigs. US, 20th C.
– a railroad engineer. US, 20th C.

Hoggers daydreaming. 20th C.

Hoggins gratification in sexual pleasure. 20th C.

Hog-grubber a low person. Late 17–19th C.
– a Thames water man. 19th C.

Hog heaven an idyllic place, or the opposite if used ironically. 20th C.

Hog Island an island in the Delaware River, Pennsylvania, once used for shipbuilding but now largely deserted swamp land. 20th C.

Hog killing weather cool autumn weather, referring to the traditional time for slaughtering the home raised pig. US, 19–20th C.

Hog-leg a pistol. US, 19–20th C.

Hog off the corn to turn pigs into the cornfield immediately after harvest to clean up the spilt grain etc. US, 20th C.

Hog-rubber a yokel or rustic, esp. an ignorant one. Mid 17th C.

Hogs the nickname of the Hampshire cricket team. 20th C.

Hog-shearing much action, little achievement. 17–18th C.

Hog's wash of the fo'c'stle head the deck hands on a merchant vessel. 20th C.

Hog-tie to hold someone down, to make helpless. 19–20th C.

Hog wallow a puddle. US, 20th C.

Hog-wash poor liquor. 18–20th C.
– trash journalism. 19–20th C.

Hog wild to go berserk. US, 20th C.

Hog-yoke a naval expression for a wooden quadrant, which was shaped like the yoke put on pigs to stop them going through narrow gaps in fences. 19th C.

Home on a pig's back to be very successful. Catch phrase from Australia and New Zealand, 20th C.

If only I had some eggs, I'd make eggs and bacon – if I had the bacon! Ironic catch phrase from the trenches during World War I.

In a pig's arse a catch phrase of incredulity. Australian, late 20th C.

In a pig's whisper very fast; in a short time. Early 19th C.

In pig pregnant. 19–20th C.

Irish as Paddy's pig/Irish as Paddy Murphy's pig very Irish indeed. From late 19th C.

It's gone over Borough Hill after Jackson's pig a local Northamptonshire expression indicating that something was lost. Mid 19–20th C. Obsolete.

Jerry Lynch a pickled pig's head. Mid 19th C.

Keep a pig to share rooms with another student. Oxford undergraduate slang. Late 19th – early 20th C.

Knight and barrow pig catch phrase applied to one considered 'more hog than gentleman', esp. one who was titled. 1780–1840.

Knight of the pigskin a jockey – based on a pigskin being slang for a saddle. Mid 19th C.

Knowing as much as a hog knows about Sunday knowing very little, ignorant. US, 20th C.

Language that would fry bacon swearing. US, 20th C.

Lie like a pig Australian term for one who tells lies. 20th C.

Like a dying pig in a thunderstorm with a sad or forlorn expression. More usually nowadays substituting 'duck' for 'pig'. Mid 19–20th C.

Like a hog in a storm out of one's senses, esp. nautical. 19th C.

Like a pig/hog – no good alive said in derision of someone unpopular through selfishness, greed etc. 16–20th C.

Like Goodyer's pig doing mischief, up to no good. Mainly Cheshire. 17–20th C.

Lipton's orphan a pig. From the illuminated sign for Lipton's bacon. Late 19–20th C.

L of C Swine lines of communication troops. World War II.

Long pig human flesh, after its supposed closeness in flavour to pork. From South Sea Islands, 19–20th C.

Make a sow's ear to cock up, make a mistake. 20th C.

Male chauvinist pig a feminist insult from the 1970s, targeting a man who treats a woman differently from the way in which he would treat a fellow male.

Mint-hog an Irish shilling. 19–20th C. Obsolete.

Mock-duck/-goose a joint of pork, stuffed and with the crackling removed to resemble a waterfowl. 19th C.

Morepork someone who is simple. 19–20th C.

More sauce than pig not much substance: more talk than action. 18–20th C.

Mortgage lifter an American settler's nickname for the pig, recognising its usefulness not only in feeding the family but in paying for the homestead as well. 19th C.

Muogh a pig. 18–20th C. Obsolete.

Murphy's face/countenance a pig's head. 19th C.

Naval pigs Naval officers. 20th C.

Never in a pig's ear never. Rhyming slang, based on 'never in a year'. 20th C.

Ogg/og a shilling – New Zealand, 20th C.

On the pig's back in Ireland and parts of Europe, some lucky mascots represent someone riding on a pig's back, often with a shamrock or a clover leaf, thus the expression represents luck. Early 20th C.

Orderly-pig army orderly officer. Early 20th C.

Pestle of pork a human leg. 19–20th C. Obsolete.

Pickled pork verbal intercourse. Rhyming slang, 'talk'. 20th C.

On the pig's back.

Pig a sixpence. 17–19th C.
– a policeman or detective. 1810 to the present.
– a pressman, according to the printing trade. 19th C.
– a ruined garment, according to tailors. 19th C.
– a segment of orange or a small piece of anything. Cockney, late 19th C.
– a chancre (a small, hard growth). 20th C.
– a girl. Beatnik slang from late 1950s.
– an elephant. Circus slang, 20th C.
– a useless horse. 20th C.
– a rugby football. Australian, 20th C.

Pig and roast army rhyming slang for toast. World War II.

Pig and whistle a ship's canteen or mess. Naval, 20th C.

Pig boat World War II naval slang for diesel-powered submarines. Derived from the experience of being downwind from one when it opened its hatches after several days of being submerged.

Pig Bridge 'The beautiful Venetian-like bridge over the Cam, where it passes St John's College, and connecting its quads. Thus called because the Johnians are styled pigs…' Mid 19–20th C. (Also known as the Isthmus of Suez – a play on the Latin *sus* for pig – and the Bridge of Grunts, 19th C.)

Pig brother a black or coloured police informant. 20th C.

Pig Command the Whitehall nickname for MAFF's (Ministry of Agriculture, Fisheries and Food) emergency control HQ during the outbreak of swine fever in the UK in 2000.

Pig-eater a 19th century term of endearment.

Pig-faced lady an Australian (particularly Tasmanian) colloquialism for the boar-fish, *c.* 1840–90.

Pig Fucker/PF Man Canadian lumberjack's term for one who looks after the tools.

Piggery a room, esp. a man's, where he does as he wishes and which can be as unclean/untidy as he pleases. 20th C.

Piggies a small child's toes. 20th C.

Pigging indulging in the act of sexual intercourse. 20th C.

Piggy the nickname for anyone in the Army or Navy called 'May'. (As in 'Chalky' White etc.) 19–20th C.
– a messman in the Navy. 20th C.

Piggy-back a child's variation of 'pick-a-back'. 19–20th C.

Piggy-stick the wooden handle of a ditching spade. Army, World War I.

Piggy-wig/piggy-wiggy a pet pig. Also used as an endearment. Mid 19–20th C.

Pig heaven a police station. 20th C.
– an idyllic place for greedy individuals. 20th C.

Pig-iron polisher Royal Navy engine room rating. 20th C.

Pig Islander an Australian term for a New Zealander, from the many wild pigs once on the islands. 19–20th C.

Pig it to share accommodation, esp. intimately. Late 19–20th C.

Pig-jump the action of jumping from a standing position from all four legs. Especially of horses. Australian, late 19th C.

Pig-market the Divinity School at Oxford University. 17–18th C.

Pig meat a whore. 20th C.

Pig-meater Australian for a steer that will not fatten. In other words, only fit for pig food. Late 19th C.

Pigmen alternative nickname for pygmies.

Pig-mill Australian term for a canteen. 20th C.

Pig-months the months of the year with an 'r' in them, i.e. September–April, when, from the old saying, it was safe to eat pork. 19–20th C. Obsolete.

Pig out to gorge to excess. Esp. American, 20th C.

Pig party a gang bang, late 20th C.

Pig-penny-horse a money box. 19–20th C.

Pig-poker swineherd. 19th C.

Pig-running from the sport at fêtes and carnivals of chasing a greased pig in the 18th and 19th C.

Pigs small potatoes. 20th C.
– abbreviation of Pig's ear, beer. (See below.)

Pigs! an expression of dismay or exasperation. 20th C.

Pigs are up military World War II slang for 'the barrage balloons are up'.

Pig-sconce someone who is considered dense or thick. 17–18th C.

Pig's ear beer, rhyming slang. Late 19–20th C.
– to make a pig's ear is to blunder, cock up. Mid 20th C.
– a mess. From the above, as a result of the blunder. Mid 20th C.
– a form of pastry. From its shape. 20th C.

Pig's ear or lug tailor's slang for a large lapel, c. 1860. Obsolete.

Pig's eye in playing cards, the ace of diamonds, from its appearance. Mid 19th C.
– something smart or favourite, as the 'cat's whiskers'. Canadian, 20th C.

Pig's foot the original version of 'my foot', meaning rubbish; an expression of disbelief. Late 19–20th C.

Pig's fry rhyming slang for 'to try'. 20th C.
– a tie, rhyming slang. From late 19th C.

Pig's-head negus soup – naval slang. 19th C.

Pigshit rubbish or nonsense. 20th C.

Pig-sick to irritate or upset. 20th C.

Pigskin a saddle, esp. in horse racing. Mid 19th C.

Pigskin artist a jockey. Australian, 20th C.

Pig's meat rubbish. Early 19th C.

Pigsney an endearment, probably derived from 'pig's eye'. 14th to early 19th C.

Pig-sticking sodomy. Canadian, 20th C.

Pig-sticker a butcher from mid 19th C.
– a sword or bayonet. Army, 19th C.

Pig-sty journalists' term for a pressroom. From mid 19th C.
– one's office or home – witty. Late 19th C.
– naval term for the wardroom. 20th C.
– police station. 20th C.

Pigtail a Chinaman, from his habit of wearing his hair in a pigtail. 19th–20th C.
– an old man, for the same reason. Early 19th C.

Pig-Tails shares in the Chartered Bank of India, Australia and China. Stock exchange, late 19th C.

Pig-tub a kitchen waste bin; from the habit of collecting swill. 19th C. Obsolete.

Pig-wigeon/-widgin an idiot or simpleton. Late 17th – late 19th C.

Pig-yoke as in hog-yoke (see above) – a naval expression for a wooden quadrant which was shaped like the yoke put on pigs to stop them going through narrow gaps in fences. 19th C.

Plastic Pig nickname for the Reliant Robin, a fibreglass 850cc three-wheeler car. Late 20th C.

Please the pigs if it's allowed to be. 17th–20th C. Obsolete. (Pigs may be a corruption of pixies.)

Pull bacon to make a rude gesture with one's fingers and nose. Mid 19th–20th C.

Pork something returned for credit or a refund, esp. to a tailor, mid 19th C.
– a woman, as the object of man's lust. 18–20th C. Obsolete.
– a pig-headed or obstinate person. 19th C.
– funds or appointments acquired by a politician to help his constituency. US, 20th C.

Pork & Beans or Pork & Beaners Portuguese soldiers or the Portuguese people; military slang from 1916. Derived from the approximate similarity of sound between the two. Pork and beans was a common tinned food in the Armed Forces.

Pork Barrel indirect reward for politicians usually associated with promoting legislation that will benefit their constituents. US, 19–20th C.

Pork-boats Worthing fishing boats, from *c.* 1850–1910.

Pork-bolter was Sussex slang for a Worthing fisherman.

Porker colloquial term for a sword, esp. naval. Probably derived from 'poker', *c.* 1685–1740.
– a Jew; derived from the Jewish abhorrence of pig meat, *c.* 1780–1900.
– a pork pie at Bootham School, mid 1920s.

Pork-knocker term for a diamond prospector in British Guiana. 20th C.

HOG THE HERO 1

Lulu was a pet Vietnamese Pot Belly, according to the *Pittsburgh Post-Gazette* in October 1998. She seemed to know that something was wrong when her owner, Jo Ann Altsman, collapsed at home with a heart attack. She went outside and past the yard, where she had never ventured before, to the side of the road. According to witnesses, there she waited until she heard a car coming, when she promptly went to the middle of the road and lay down. The car stopped, the driver got out and Lulu got up and led him into the house from where he called the emergency services, thus saving Jo Ann's life. Eat your heart out, Lassie!

Porkopolis in the 1860s, Cincinnati, Ohio, was the main centre for the hog trade in the USA but lost its crown to Chicago when the Civil War closed access to the city.

Pork-pie an abbreviation for pork-pie hat, a man's hat popular in the mid-1850s.

Pork sword the human phallus. 20th C.

Porky a butcher, especially a pork butcher. Early 20th C. Obsolete.
– a Jew. Early 20th C. Obsolete.

Porky pies porkies – lies. Rhyming slang, 20th C.

Pull the wrong pig by the ear to cock up/make a mistake. *c.* 1540–1870. (Sometimes 'get' was used instead of 'pull' and 'sow' substituted for 'pig'.)

Rabbit and pork to talk. Rhyming slang, thus to 'rabbit', meaning talk, chatter. 20th C.

River hog/pig Canadian for a lumber worker engaged in working on the river. 20th C.

Road-hog an inconsiderate road user or motorist. Originally from the 1890s – almost as old as the car!

Roast pork to talk. Rhyming slang, 20th C.
– a dining fork. Army rhyming slang, World War II.

The original road-hog? An Edwardian postcard.

Robin hog a police constable. Early 18th C.

Rough as a pig's breakfast very uncouth. New Zealand slang. 20th C.

Ruff peck bacon. 16–18th C.

Rum ruff peck Westphalia ham. 16–17th C.

Sand hog an Irish navvy working in New York on the tunnel between Manhattan and New Jersey. 18th C.

Sea-pork whale meat. 19–20th C.

Seeley's pigs pig iron. From the name of the MP for Lincoln who disclosed in the 19th C that government dockyards were 'half paved with iron pigs'.

Sky-hog a low-flying airman. Mid 20th C.

Slice off the same bacon someone or something that is very similar to another. US, 20th C.

Sling tail pickled pork. 19th C.

Small pigs Petty officers. 20th C.

Snags sausages. Australian, 20th C.

Snore like a pig in the sun to snore loudly or persistently. Mid 19–20th C.

Snork/snorker a sausage. Australian/New Zealand, 20th C.

Snout a hogshead. 18th C.

Son of a sow/son of a sow-gelder a bastard. 17–19th C.

Soor an abusive expression derived from the Hindustani for 'pig'. Army slang, 19th C.

Sow-belly Army slang for salt pork and bacon. Late 19th C.

Sow's baby a suckling pig. 17–20th C. Obsolete.
– a sixpence, derived from hog meaning shilling (see 'hog' above).
  Mid 19th C.

Squeaker a young pig. Mid 19th C.

Snags, snorks, snorkers or strays, at least to those from Australia.

Squeal bacon. 19–20th C. Obsolete.

Squealer a pork sausage – tramp's slang, 20th C.

Steam pig anything otherwise undefined. Railway slang. 20th C.

Still sow someone who is sly, cunning, from the proverb, 'the still sow eats up all the draff'. 16–17th C.

Stray a sausage. Australian naval, 20th C.

Subtle as a dead pig earlier version of 'cunning as a dead pig'. 17–18th C.

Swine mixture a composition of mashed sardines, cocoa and Nestle's tinned milk, created at Bishop's Stortford College between the wars. The purpose was not explained.

Swine-up an argument or quarrel. Late 19th to early 20th C.

Swing-tail a pig. Late 18th to mid 19th C.

Teach a pig to play on the flute similar to 'pigs might fly', in other words, to do the impossible. 19th C.

That's another hog off the corn one less person to feed because they have been fed elsewhere. US, 20th C.

That's the way the hog bladder bounces something that is inevitable. US, 20th C.

The bandmaster a pig's head. Nautical. 20th C.

The Flying Pig railway slang for freight trains bringing bacon to London. Mid 20th C.

The gentleman who pays the rent a pig. Irish. Mid 19–20th C. Obsolete.

The Hog Governor the nickname given to US politician Thomas Jefferson in 1780.

The Pig Blue Boar Hotel, Cambridge. Undergraduate slang, 20th C.

The Pig & Tinder Box a comic interpretation of the sign for the Elephant & Castle, London, c. 1820–90. ('Toddle to the Pig and Tinder-Box… a little drap of comfort there', Egan, 1821.)

The Pig & Whistle Light Infantry the Highland Light Infantry, from the badge of the 71st Regiment of Foot (1880s) which showed an elephant and a hunting horn. 19–20th C. Obsolete.

The Pig & Whistle Line Chidley Dike. The railway line between Cheltenham and Southampton Docks. 20th C. Obsolete.

The Pigs military nickname for two 19th C regiments; 76th Foot Regiment and 2nd Battalion of West Riding Regiment.

The Pork & Lard railwaymen's slang for the St Ives to Ely line. 20th C.

There comes a pig to be killed expression of disbelief. Early 20th C.

There were four turds for dinner – stir turd (hog's face), held turd (feet), treat turd (chitterlings) and must-turd (mustard). 19th C.

They'll come again as Goodyer's pigs did i.e. never. It is not recorded who Goodyer was although the name may derive from the Scottish word for grandfather. Mid 17th to mid 18th C.

365 eggs and bacon. Travelling salesman's term for standard B&B breakfast. 19–20th C.

Tiger streaky bacon. Working man's slang. Late 19th C.

To bring one's pigs to a fine market to do well, succeed. Now obsolete. 17–20th C.
– ironically, the opposite: to fail, to manage badly. 18–20th C.

To choke on your bacon to be over-enthusiastic, go overboard. (Relates back to the Spanish Inquisition when Philip II of Spain was so keen to demonstrate that he was not a heretic that he almost choked to death gorging on bacon.) 19–20th C.

To drive one's hogs/pigs to market to snore. 18–20th C.

To go to pigs and whistles to be bankrupted or ruined. Scottish, from *c.* 1780.

To have been born at Hogs Norton to be uncouth, rude. Mid 16–19th C.

To hog to grab or to eat or drink in a greedy way. From early 20th C.
– to have sex. Mid 19–20th C.
– to sleep, especially accompanied by snoring. 20th C.
– to behave like a road-hog. 20th C.
– to cut a horse's main short, or to remove it completely (US).
– to cause an arch, 20th C.
– to monopolise, 20th C.
– to sow corn on unploughed land (US) 20th C.
– to cut timber in a wasteful manner (US) 20th C.

Too many pigs for the tits not enough to go round. 20th C.

To pig to ruin something completely. Tailors' slang. 20th C.

Trilbys pig's trotters. Yorkshire slang from turn of 20th C.

Trotters nickname for Bolton Wanderers Football Club. 20th C.

Underground hog the chief engineer. Canadian railway, 20th C.

When pigs fly i.e. never. 17th C to the present.

Whistle pig a groundhog, a small American rodent. 20th C.

Whole-hogger a politician who embraces all the issues. 19–20th C.

Yankee Pigs term for the Americans during the Spanish-American war of 1898.

Before we leave the world of slang and insults, it is worth looking to the British Houses of Parliament where the definition of 'unparliamentary language' is a forever shifting landscape, a quagmire just waiting for the inexperienced and unwary to take a wrong step. For example, in 1992 'porkies' was added to the list of the unacceptable by the then Speaker, Bernard Weatherill. The Labour MP for Workington, Dale Campbell-Savours, was asked to withdraw the expression, which he had used in relation to a Tory Minister and his pronouncements. Most other words relating to the pig have already long since been banned at Westminster and MPs must find other ways to describe their honourable friends without the benefit of any of the splendid expressions listed above.

FAIRY PIGS IN THE ISLE OF MAN

The Isle of Man has an unusual reputation for harbouring a whole host of fairy pigs, some benign, some aggressive. These pigs tend to haunt particular roads and bridges around the island. 'Ark Sonney', as one is named, is said to be a lucky omen for those who meet it. Another, which can apparently be seen wearing a rather charming red hat in the area of Glenfaba, is reputed to be quite harmless. In contrast, however, the large, pale coloured boar said to haunt Grenaby Bridge is believed to be far from harmless, as it carries off travellers up river to a cave near Barrule and from there into the underworld. Many of these fairy pigs are described as having large, frilly ears.

TRUFFLE HUNTING

The old Pig said to the little pigs,
'In the forest is truffles and mast,
Follow me then, all ye little pigs,
Follow me fast!'

– Walter de la Mare (1873–1956)

Black truffles and white truffles, a form of fungus which grows below ground, are highly prized as gastronomic delights and aphrodisiacs, particularly in countries where good food is richly appreciated such as France and Italy. Retail prices can exceed £1,000 per kilo! The truffles grow around the roots of young broad-leaved trees such as oaks and beeches – provided, of course, that the spores are present in the soil. They are notoriously difficult to find and harvest, resulting in the astronomic prices for these highly prized, if ugly, tubers. Pigs (and more recently dogs) are used to hunt for them. The pig has even been referred to as 'the Christopher Columbus of the truffle'.

A pig's senses are concentrated in its snout. It has an acute sense of smell, surpassing anything we can muster and it is this that allows the pig to find truffles where man would walk by. The truffle has a distinctive, musk-like scent, from which its reputation as an aphrodisiac arises, as it contains a pheromone, or more particularly, androstenol, a sex pheromone also found in pigs, used by them to attract a mate. It is similar to the scent of a human armpit and is recognised as a sexual stimulant. Thus female pigs are considered to be much better at truffle hunting than males.

The problem with truffle hunting with pigs is that once detected, the sow is anxious to get to the prized fungus herself and nature put most of the digging power in the pig's snout with the support of some very strong neck muscles. Thus the pig can switch very quickly from sniffing to excavating and as the truffle is only a few inches below the surface, a battle can ensue to ensure that the truffle is safely harvested and not consumed by the porker. One solution is to muzzle the pig and to train her by quickly diverting her attention from the truffle and rewarding her with some less expensive titbit. An alternative method is amusingly described by Peter Mayle in his book *Toujours Provence*, where the local truffle-hunting

➤

expert is training up a Vietnamese Pot Belly, a smaller and thus much more tractable pig. Good news, perhaps, for all those who bought them in the eighties as pets and now wonder what to do with them – if only they could find some truffles! Incidentally, the pig as a species is ideally suited to digging with its snout and can even close its nostrils at such times so as to prevent the ingress of dirt.

Another rather nice tale from France concerns the selection of your truffle hunter. The recommendation is to ask the farmer the price of his pig as you manoeuvre your way into the sty. Once he has committed himself, take out a small truffle from your pocket, discreetly squash it under foot to release the scent and then stand back and watch the reaction. A good specimen will respond immediately – but by then it is too late for the farmer to up the ante!

An old French postcard showing a truffle-hunting team.

The main truffle hunting areas are the Perigord region of France and parts of Italy, with the season running from October through to March or between the first frost and the last. But do not despair. Summer truffles can be found in much the same way in many parts of Britain, although their price is lower than the Black Diamonds from France. They have been successfully harvested in the Forest of Dean and near Wotton-under-Edge in Gloucestershire, in the Savernake Forest in Wiltshire and one man, at least, is finding a lot in Scotland. In the nineteenth century, they were frequently harvested in London's Royal Parks and in the New Forest.

Modern scientists are trying to find ways of regulating the truffle harvest. In Italy and France, saplings are being sold with roots that have been sprayed with the spores of truffles, with the sales pitch that, in two to three years, you can start harvesting your own tubers without having to search for them. In 1990, it was reported that at the University of Manchester Institute of Science and Technology they had developed a microchip sensor to sniff out truffles. In trials in Bordeaux, the high-tech chip was four times more efficient at finding specially secreted truffles than a locally trained dog but comparisons were not offered against the pig. Somehow, wandering around the forest with a glorified metal detector seems to lack the charm of the bond between man and another intelligent beast hunting together. In Oregon, USA, it was reported a few years ago that two elderly gentlemen had dispensed with all aids and developed their own sense of smell to such an extent that, by crawling around the forest floor on their bellies, they could detect the elusive erotic scent themselves. Self-discipline, if not age, meant that they were less likely to gobble the raw tubers straight down.

Some scientists are using the pig's love of truffles in a different way. In 1990, it was reported that a UK animal feed producer, Pauls Agriculture, was synthetically recreating the smell and taste of truffles as an additive to pig food, in order to encourage the pigs to eat more! The pigs in question are those hybrids now being kept out of doors and whose appetites contract when the weather turns cold. How long can it be before such flavourings start finding their way into crisps and pot noodles, especially bearing in mind their aphrodisiac claims?

DRUG DETECTION

In much the same way as the Perigord truffle hunters, police in Lower Saxony in Germany experimented in the 1980s with a wild boar, Luise, who was trained to sniff out drugs. Her advanced sense of smell meant that she could detect illegal drugs such as cannabis or heroin hidden inside other containers.

The idea came to Werner Franke, a commissioner in charge of the dog-handling unit at Hanover, after he had visited a local country park and seen wild boar there. 'I wondered what animals we could use to supplement our dogs,' he said in a newspaper report. 'Wild boar seemed the best bet.'

Luise was three months old when she came to him and was trained inside eight months. 'We use the same method as with the dogs. When she finds a container of hashish or cocaine, she's rewarded with a biscuit. Her sense of smell is at least as acute as a dog's,' said Franke. 'And she's clearly better with anything buried. A dog is only good for fifteen minutes hard scenting, then its nose overloads and it gets bored. Luise will keep going all day.'

So, why are redundant sniffer dogs not roaming the *strasse* of Germany? Well, truth to tell, the Lower Saxony police retired Luise after a few months because 'she was bad for their image'. Sensitive to jibes of '*Schwein!*' already, the Hanoverian constables apparently felt that her presence was just playing into the hands of the cruel public and persuaded the commissioner that the less efficient hounds should be reinstated.

Then in 1991, Customs officials in Britain, who had studied the German experiment with a view perhaps to adopting pig sniffers at Heathrow Airport, claimed that pigs were quicker to train than dogs and less likely to become addicted to snorting the dubious substances.

Meanwhile, what happened to Luise? She took to the media circuit around Germany as a 'celebrity', even dropping in to join the Hanover Opera Company one evening. In 1987 she starred in a film called *Blutrausch* (Blood Frenzy) as a porcine private eye and she has appeared on television more than seventy times.

More recently in New Jersey, USA, one Ferris E. Lucas has joined forces with sheriff's officer Matt Jagusak in the eternal search for illegal narcotics.

➤

Ferris E. Lucas is, in fact, a Vietnamese Pot Belly and has the admiration of his 'pardner'; Matt Jagusak says that Ferris's sense of smell is about one million times better than a human's and is only beaten by that of a blood-hound. In his opinion his Vietnamese Pot Belly is the best there is in terms of drug detection.

The superior detection skills of pigs have also been utilised to help in the location of landmines.

PROTECTION FROM SNAKES

Wild boar have handed on a valuable attribute to their domesticated cousins. The one thing pigs are not afraid of is snakes. Both wild and tame will eat the most poisonous of snakes with rarely a problem. The pig's skin is thick and difficult for the snake to penetrate and even when it does, the chances are that the poisonous venom will be injected into the pig's layer of fat rather than into the bloodstream or nervous system.

Pigs use this advantage to enable them to supplement their diet and will happily consume snakes. They do not make the mistake of going in snout first since that is an area very vulnerable to snake bites but instead will rush the snake and trample it to death before gobbling it up. In the West Indies, the pig is credited with dealing with more snakes even than the mongoose, the traditional snake killer. In America in the 1870s, pigs were even employed to clear a district of rattlesnakes, which they did most successfully.

In eastern Spain, pigs are encouraged to feed on the local species of viper, as the snake's venom is said to enhance the flavour of the hams to an even greater extent than eating peaches benefits the taste of the pigs of Virginia.

Louis Robinson in *Wild Traits in Tame Animals* (1897), wondered on the subject of pigs: 'What if, after all, he was the real Saint Patrick, who cleared Ireland of snakes?'

SOW STATUESQUE!

In Pennsylvania, down by a small river at Chadds Ford, you will find the Brandywine River Museum, renowned for exhibiting, amongst others, artistic works by three generations of the Wyeth family. In the grounds of the museum is a lovely bronze of a full-sized sitting pig, Helen, the work of André Harvey. Enough in itself to justify a trip to this region.

SOW INSULTING!

A quick and witty response is a wonderful thing and one that most of us only think of when it is too late; Dorothy Parker was a famous exception to this rule:

Age before beauty.

– Clare Boothe Luce (on meeting Dorothy Parker in a doorway)

Pearls before swine!

– Dorothy Parker (sailing majestically through the door)

King Henry VIII was known to be open to insult from time to time and the following description was assigned to him by Martin Luther: '… a pig, an ass, a dunghill, the spawn of an adder, a basilisk, a lying buffoon, a mad fool with a frothy mouth… a lubberly ass… a frantic madman…' One gets the impression that the Tudor monarch was none too popular. Yet the king himself could be self-deprecating too, for in 1534 he ordered for his personal use a supply of notepaper with a watermark depicting a pig wearing a tiara, thus characterising himself as that brutish creature wearing a bejewelled crown.

Swine Sayings

If you would live well for a week, kill a hog;
if you would live well for a month, marry;
if you would live well all your life, turn priest.

A saying from times past when the priest could expect a good living and high respect. Another variation goes:

If you would be happy for a week kill a pig;
if you would be happy for a month take a wife;
but if you would be happy all your life, plant a garden.

You can pook and you can shove,
but a Sussex pig he wun't be druv.

Implying that those from Sussex are pigheaded.

You May Push Me
You May Shuv
But I'm Hanged
If I'll Be Druv

An old postcard utilising a variation on the Sussex saying.

— 40 —

He's like an Irishman's pig – he'll neither lead nor drive.

Lancashire saying from the end of the 19th century.

The race of pigs is expressly given by nature to set forth a banquet.

Roman saying. Pig meat was always recognised for its richness.

Well-known Sayings

To buy a pig in a poke.

From *c.* 1300, when it was common practice at market to sell small pigs in a sack, i.e. a blind bargain. From the same transaction comes '*Letting the cat out of the bag*' when an unscrupulous vendor would substitute a cat for a pig and be found out when the purchaser inspected the contents of the bag.

You cannot make a silk purse out of a sow's ear.

In other words, you cannot make something if you do not have the right materials. This was often applied in times past to persons of low breeding, implying that no amount of education or social pretensions could turn a low-born being into a gentleman or lady. A modern twist to this ancient saw is '*To make a pig's ear of it*' or in other words to receive some silk in order to make your purse but to botch the job so completely that it turns out looking like a pig's ear.

The Kune Kune from New Zealand (the name means short and round in Maori) showing the two wattles hanging from the neck, a feature found on many of the breed.

To be led up (down) the garden path.

This relates to the time when pigs were kept in the cottage sty, where they would remain from the day of their arrival until their final hour. One can only imagine their delight at being let out for some apparent freedom, though this would only have happened as they were led out of the sty to meet the local village pig killer. Coaxed and handled gently so as to avoid undue stress (although such niceties did not always take place), the animal was truly led on a journey of deception – summed up in the phrase we remember today, even though the act it relates to is largely long forgotten.

'The Pig Slaughter' Jean-François Millet 1814–75

To save your bacon.

Dating back to the 17th century, this saying relates to the time when heretics could expect to be burnt at the stake and thus a judicious claim to orthodoxy could avoid the effects of smoke and fire.

Do not cast your pearls before swine.

Do not give something beautiful or precious to someone who cannot appreciate it. This biblical quotation comes from Matthew 7.6, The Sermon on the Mount. There is some argument among scholars as to the translation from the Hebrew with the suggestion that, instead of pearls, the original meaning was marguerites – a name for the oxeye daisy – but the intended message is the same, whatever item of beauty is cast before swine.

To go the whole hog.

Originally an American expression from around 1828, when it became popular during Andrew Jackson's presidential campaign. It was in use in Britain by 1850. It may be a derisory reference to the Moslem faith and the recorded instance of certain Mohammedans interpreting their instructions to the letter as alluded to in William Cowper's poem (*The Love of the World Reproved*, or *Hypocrisy Detected*, 1779):

> But for one piece they thought it hard
> From the whole hog to be debarred.

Alternatively, 'hog' was once a well-known term for a shilling, especially in Ireland and 'to go the whole hog' may have referred to blowing the entire sum in one go.

❖

To bring home the bacon.

To succeed at a stated task. This might refer to the winning of the Dunmow Flitch (see page 68) or one of the prizes from the country fairs and fêtes.

❖

Hamming it up.

Playing to the gallery, over-acting. This is related to 'ham actor' and dates back to the last quarter of the nineteenth century. In those days, there was no cold cream to help clean off the actor's make up or greasepaint. Instead, they used blocks of ham fat. Individuals who over-acted were thus deemed real actors who must therefore need to use lots of ham fat. Although the origins of the term are mostly long forgotten, the words are so evocative that the expression is widely recognised in the English-speaking world.

❖

Pigs see the wind.

Pigs are recognised as having a sixth sense and can foretell storms before humans are aware of the change in weather. At such times, they are seen to run around excitedly, often with straw in their mouths with which to build a nest.

❖

Some Less Familiar Sayings

Dogs look up to you,
Cats look down on you,
Pigs is equal!

Undeniably true! Of Gloucestershire origin. A variation of this is often credited to a quotation by Sir Winston Churchill but in this instance he borrowed it from the peasantry.

❖

Great cry and little wool…

… as the Devil said when he sheared the hogs. Similar to 'all talk and no do', in other words, used contemptuously of someone who does not deliver what he promises.

❖

Higgledy piggledy.

In a sprawling heap, at sixes and sevens, much as a sleeping litter of pigs may be seen. From the 16th century.

❖

Hogging the limelight.

Pushing oneself forward at the expense of others.

❖

Pig ignorant.

Why? I have yet to meet a member of the species who could not be described as knowing and cunning. Of 20th century origin.

❖

To stare like a stuck pig.

Open-mouthed in astonishment, as a dead pig might appear.

❖

As independent as a hog on ice.

Very confident and self-assured. Of greater use in America than Britain, although the origin may be Scottish, perhaps arising from the terms used in the sport of curling.

Pigs in clover.

Similar implications to the phrase *nouveau riche*, meaning people coming into wealth and not knowing how to handle it. 'A sort of pig in clover' appears in a letter written by D. H. Lawrence to Aldous Huxley, dated 27 March 1928, describing the playwright, Arnold Bennett.

Faint heart never kissed a pig.

Twentieth century saying, not frequently disproven.

Faint heart never kissed a pig...

Piggy in the middle.

Torn between two extremes; unable to satisfy both. From the children's game where a ball is thrown from one to another with a third standing between them, with the object of preventing 'piggy' from catching the ball.

To get the wrong sow by the ear.

To come to the wrong conclusion, or 'to get hold of the wrong end of the stick'.

To have the right sow by the ear.

To have hit upon the right answer or solution.

Unless your bacon you would mar,
Kill not your pig without the R.

From the days before refrigeration, when it was considered safe to eat pork only during the months September to April. Surprisingly, a number of people still adhere to this adage, albeit probably subconsciously.

❖

In a pig's ear/eye/arse.

Nonsense or rubbish.

❖

Like a pig needs a hip pocket.

Totally unnecessary.

❖

A pig used to dirt turns up its nose at rice boiled in milk.

Japanese proverb.

❖

Draff good enough for hogs.

The English version, said of those who refuse something that is fine in favour of something that is coarse.

❖

To be on the pig's back.

To be doing well, prospering.

❖

To hear as a hog in harvest.

In one ear and out of the other. Dates back to the 17th century.

❖

To go to pigs and whistles.

A Scottish expression meaning to be ruined, to have gone to pot. Some suggest that the various pubs called The Pig & Whistle may be named after this expression but if so it seems incredible that anyone would so name a hostelry and expect to attract trade and make a profit!

❖

To drive one's hog to market.

To snore.

To call pigs.

To snore.

❖

I think you were born at Hogs Norton.

A reproof to a coarse or ill-mannered person. Hogs Norton is a mythical village 'where pigs play on the organ'. More recently it was a place used by radio broadcaster Gillie Potter (in the 1930s) as the setting for a series of tales of unlikely events.

❖

Stealing acorns from a blind pig.

Something that's easily done – a piece of cake.

❖

A good fat pig to last you all the year,
A pocketful of money and a cellar full of beer!

A popular ditty used to wish someone a Happy New Year. Found in greetings cards at the end of the 19th century.

❖

Not fit to roll with a pig.

Someone so described is coarse and uncouth – the lowest of the low!

If that don't beat a pig a-pecking!

Something that is quite amazing: unbelievable. Mainly used in America.

To pig together.

To share space with another person to whom you are not married.

A pig's whisper.

A very short period of time. The expression appears in Charles Dickens's *Pickwick Papers*: 'You'll find yourself in bed in something less than a pig's whisper.'

Bartholomew Pig.

A description of a fat person, after the custom at the St Bartholomew Fair in London to spit-roast a whole, very fat pig for consumption by the populace.

High on the hog.

A person with extravagant tastes. It is said to have derived from the 19th century British Army where enlisted men and NCOs ate the cheaper cuts of pork but the officers had the loin, located higher up the body.

The still sow eats the draff.

Someone who is wise and cunning and thus does not converse during meal-times but quietly carries on eating so as to obtain more than his share.

To bring your pigs to a fine market.

To have managed one's business in a poor way or to have made a bad bargain. This dates back to mediaeval times when goods were bartered and the pig was the most common item of currency with which to pay the rent etc.

To follow one about like an Anthony pig.

Used of someone who is a hanger-on. It derives from stories of Saint Anthony, the patron saint of swineherds. After various exploits concerning the healing of sick animals, the pigs belonging to Saint Anthony, primarily runts, were allowed the run of anywhere they went without harm and were identified by a bell around the neck. They were, in effect, almost pet pigs and would follow people about in the hope of receiving some edible reward.

A pig that has two owners is sure to die of hunger.

Sooner or later, one will assume that the other is taking care of things and vice versa.

To take two boars in one covert.

Of Latin origin, with the same meaning as 'to kill two birds with one stone'.

A poor man's cow and an alewife's sow are always well fed.

Old English proverb.

The young pig grunts like the old sow.

Youth learns from older generations.

Everyone basteth the fat hog's arse while the lean one burneth.

People suck up to the rich and ignore the poor, who might benefit from the extra attention.

A pretty pig makes an ugly old sow.

Very few humans manage to make it to old age with the fair looks of youth. Many people, even today, are attracted to the cuteness of a bright, shiny piglet and should bear this advice in mind before choosing one as a pet.

Better my hog dirty home than no hog at all.

Another old fashioned expression similar to 'better late than never'.

He does not lose his alms who gives it to his pig.

Old French proverb indicating that it is better to invest income than to consume it.

He loves bacon well who licks it off the swine-sty door.

He is completely committed to his task.

❖

Like a hog, he does no good 'til he dies.

Many believe that pigs are only good for producing meat and that, unlike other farm animals, they are not beasts of burden nor will they supply milk or wool.

French advertising poster from 1925.

The hog is never good but when he is in the dish.

A variation.

Poets and pigs are not appreciated until they are dead.

A slightly different approach from Italy.

Little pigs eat great potatoes.

Providence often puts a large potato in a little pig's way.

Irish and English proverbs of similar meaning.

Ne'er lose a hog for a half-pennyworth of tar.

It is by no means certain that 'hog' here relates to the swine as to the sheep – as 'hog' or 'hogget' also relates to a shearling sheep in its first year and tar is more likely to be used on sheep than pigs. Further complications arise when one considers that the saying may have applied to a 'hogshead', a barrel with a capacity of around fifty-two gallons.

You cannot make a horn of a pig's tail.

With variations, such as 'shaft' in place of 'horn'. Used in both England and Denmark, it is similar to making a silk purse from a sow's ear for although a curled tail is the same shape as a hunting horn, nothing can make it perform the same function.

Pigs grow fat where lambs would starve.

Cut your coat according to your cloth. Just because one thing will not work does not mean another is not ideally suited to the circumstances.

Pigs grunt about everything and nothing.

Do not believe everything you are told.

Pigs love that lie together.

Given a lack of constraint, certain people will give in to basic urges if circumstances allow.

Swine, women and bees cannot be turned.

The term 'pigheaded' is aptly made, since once a pig is determined to take a course of action, precious little will alter it. Certainly, a swarm of bees is much the same, so one must assume that the reference to women might also be true!

The first pig, but the last whelp, is the best.

A 17th century observation turned into a proverb.

The sow loves bran better than roses.

French proverb, in much the same mould as casting pearls before swine.

To steal the pig and give the feet to God.

A derisory expression indicating that one cannot effectively salve one's conscience by doing a good deed using the results of a crime. There are versions of this in both Italian and Spanish.

Turned the pigs into grass.

A French proverb indicating that the subject has been changed or a diversion caused.

Nothing compared with Parmeno's sow.

This is a Latin proverb with a story behind it. According to Plutarch, Parmeno was an excellent mimic of the grunting and squeaking of a pig. A rival, in trying to go one better, performed a similar feat on stage, but the crowd was biased towards Parmeno and said that the upstart's efforts were 'nothing compared with Parmeno's sow'. However, the rival had concealed a real pig beneath his cloak and the crowd had rejected the real thing in favour of Parmeno's mimicry.

Where there is no hook, to be sure there will hang no bacon.

You cannot do the job without the tools. Old English proverb.

Poor and pert, like the parson's pig.

This relates to the paying of tithes (taxes) to the church, when the smallest in the litter would be the one destined for the priest.

We don't kill a pig every day.

Old Lincolnshire proverb. The killing of the pig was almost a festival for family and friends as items such as the offal, which would not keep, were shared out. Thus the meaning is that we do not have a holiday or feast every day.

THE WILD PIGS OF HAMPSTEAD

During the 19th century a widely believed fable arose which has much in common with the modern urban myth in New York, concerning the presence of gigantic alligators in the sewers of that city, apparently resulting from the flushing away of redundant pets down the lavatory.

Recorded by sociologist Henry Mayhew, the London version runs that a pregnant sow gets into the sewer system below Hampstead and successfully raises her litter, which forms the basis of a colony of wild and terrifying swine below the streets of London. They remain forever subterranean because the River Fleet forms an impenetrable barrier, but stay alive by feeding from the waste and sewage passing by. Physically, they revert to long, lean beasts, like wild boar, with wild eyes and huge tusks. Despite never actually being witnessed, Victorian sewer men were said to have believed in them implicitly.

Like a pig's tail, going all day and nothing done at night.

Lancashire proverb dating back to the 17th century.

Silence in the pigmarket, and let the old sow have a grunt.

Briefly used proverb dating from the late 19th century.

Pigs may whistle, but they have an ill mouth for it.

An alternative to 'pigs might fly'. 'Pigs will never play well on the flute, teach them as long as you like.' C. H. Spurgeon, 1880.

Excuse my pig, he's a friend.

Said in reproof of someone who belches in public. Modern.

Have you pigs in your belly?

The 18th century equivalent.

Child's pig but father's bacon.

Children might be told that an orphan pig or lamb was theirs to look after but when the time came for slaughter or market, their parents kept the benefit of the final transaction.

As cunning as a dead pig but not half so honest.

From the expression of guile on a dead pig's face.

Whom God loves, his bitch brings forth pigs.

A litter of pigs was worth far more than a litter of puppies: rarely true today. Pigs also provided food whereas dogs did not.

The hog never looks up to him that threshes down the acorns.

The pig does not mind who feeds him, as long as he is fed.

It is ill to drive black hogs in the dark.

If you cannot see what you are doing, how can you do it?

What can you expect from a hog but a grunt?

Said in reproof of anyone using coarse or foul language.

He who does not kill hogs, will not get black puddings.

Black puddings, made primarily from the blood of the pig, were only available to those who killed and bled the pig because it had to be as fresh as possible. Spanish; 19th century proverb.

The last man that he killed keeps hogs in Hinckley field.

Spoken of a boaster or coward.

Lubberland, where the pigs run about ready roasted, and cry, Come eat me!

A derisory maxim, implying that there is never something for nothing and that to achieve something, one must work for it.

More sauce than pig.

Said of a meal when little meat but much sauce is found, i.e. there is little of substance to the matter in hand.

He that hath one hog, makes him fat; and he that hath one son makes him a fool.

With only one thing to concentrate on, the chances are that it will be spoiled.

Give to a pig when it grunts and a child when it cries, and you will have a fine pig and a bad child.

Chinese version.

As pleased as a pig with two tails.

A contented pig will swish its tail about more than a dog wags its tail.

As snug as a pig in pea straw.

Early version of 'as snug as a bug in a rug'.

Couch a hogshead.

To go to sleep; 16th century.

The worst hog often gets the best pear.

As much as it goes against natural justice, the bully or despot usually has the best of things, at least for a time.

Right, Roger, your sow is good mutton.

Going along with what someone says, even though it is obviously not true or possible.

Like a sow playing on a trump.

Lacking in grace.

A sow teaching Minerva.

A Latin reference, equivalent to teaching your grandmother to suck eggs. Minerva was the Roman goddess of wisdom.

As meet as a sow to bear a saddle.

It does not fit or suit the subject.

The swine's gone through it.

Spoken of a marriage which does not take place, from the old Scottish superstition that if a pig comes between a man and his intended bride, they will never be married. Proverb from the 18th century.

Little knows the fat sow what the lean does mean.

In 1852, this expression was used thus by E. Fitzgerald:

'The Fat Sow knoweth not what the Lean one thinks ... Swollen Wealth is well enacted by the fat Sow reclining in her sty, as a Dowager in an opera-box, serenely unconscious of all her kindred's leanness without.'

He that does not love a woman, sucked a sow.

Saying from the 17th century, implying that homosexuality arises from an unnatural upbringing.

Safe as a sow in the gutter.

In mediaeval times, before the era of land enclosure, pigs roamed the streets of towns and villages, acting as mobile dustbins and a pig in the gutter was as natural a situation as one could find.

Who singest like a bird called swine?

Who's not singing in tune?

He that has sheep, swine and bees, sleep he, wake he, he may thrive.

Quoted as being 'an olde saying' in the 16th century, when the requirements for life may have been a little simpler than today's.

To sell one's bacon.

To sell one's body, especially said of mercenaries.

The Latins call me Porcus.

Said of someone who is boastful or too clever for their own good. The saying derives from an old fable of a meeting between a wolf and a pig. The story runs that the animals meet and the wolf makes it clear that the pig is destined to become his next meal. But the pig admonishes him, pointing out that the day is Friday and as a good Roman Catholic, the wolf should not be indulging his appetite for meat that day. The wolf regretfully agrees and they fall into an amiable stroll together through the woods. The wolf comments that the pig is a clever fellow and queries the number of names given to his species. 'Yes,' said the pig, 'I am called swine, grunter, hog, and I know not what besides. The Latins call me *porcus*.' ' "Porpus", do they?' said the wolf. 'Well, porpoise is a fish, and we may eat fish on a Friday,' and devoured him without another word.

It takes a good breed of pig to eat acorns.

Old Gloucestershire saying. You cannot fatten pigs on the free harvest of the forest floor alone.

Never buy pigs in an East wind.

A practical saying, since it is unwise to buy young pigs to fatten on a cold day. Weaners are especially vulnerable and will rarely prosper after a day in a cold and draughty market.

Where the sun does not come, the doctor does.

A similar saw about pig keeping.

An Essex boar belonging to Mr Fisher Hobbs of Marks Hall, Coggeshall – winner at the Royal Show in 1843.

Pigs will prosper that lie close together.

Keeping your stock warm in social groups is good pig husbandry.

A swine doth sooner than a cow
Bring an ox to the plough.

An old Gloucestershire saying, extolling the virtues of a pig on the farm which will prepare land for cultivation quicker than a cow.

When it comes to pain, hunger and thirst, a rat is a pig is a dog is a boy.

Rallying cry of the extreme fringe of the animal rights movement.

As welcome as a pork chop in a synagogue.

Fairly unwelcome, obviously. Modern.

A pig in the parlour is still a pig.

Someone or something dressed up as another is still the original.

Lead a pig to the Rhine, it remains a pig.

The German equivalent is equally expressive.

You can put lipstick on a pig, but it's still a pig.

President (then Senator) Barack Obama got into hot water with this analogy in the 2008 presidential campaign, as the words came out within just a couple of days of the statement by Sarah Palin (the Republican vice-presidential candidate) that the only difference between 'a pit bull and a hockey mom is lipstick'. The Republicans complained that Obama was likening their chosen one to a pig.

As Irish as Paddy's pig.

It was inconceivable that an Irish country cottage was not home to a pig. The New York *Sun* claimed that the pig in question was Roscommon King, owned by Paddeen Slavin and shown in London in 1895. It is also claimed that the reference comes from an Irish song of the same name from the 19th century.

Pigs are either muck or money.

Pig farming has almost always been undertaken on low overheads. When prices were good, lots of farmers took to fattening pigs but when the prices fell due to over-production, they quickly got out – a system known as the pig cycle.

It will rain if pigs appear uneasy and rub themselves in dust.

Traditional weather lore.

Old pigs have hard snouts.

A derisory assertion, indicating that in business, it is usually the older person who is 'hard-nosed'.

It is a lazy pig that will not eat ripe pears.

Soft, juicy pears are among the easiest things for a pig to eat. Said of someone who is considered to be excessively lazy.

Feed a pig and you will have a hog.

Those aspects of pigs which man despises are often inflicted on the pig by the way he is kept.

As a sow fills, the pigwash sours.

As a hungry man eats, the meat loses its relish.

A barren sow is never good to pigs.

The only reason to keep a pig to maturity was to breed from it and a barren sow is no use to that end.

From rip of boar, though very sore,
There is not much to fear;
But bad the smart from horn of hart,
'Twill bring thee to thy bier.

Hunting proverb.

As sick as a Vietnam pig.

A local variation on 'as sick as a parrot', as sometimes heard in the Hull area.

A hog that's bemir'd endeavours to bemire others.

Said of someone who has been found out and who then tries to implicate others in return for a lighter punishment. From the 18th century.

A hog upon trust, grunts till he's paid for.

Reminders for payment are only noticed whilst the debt is outstanding.

As noisy as two pigs under a gate.

A pig, when accidentally trapped, will squeal uncontrollably and the noise is very loud. However, two pigs do not produce twice the noise level. Scientists put the increase at around twenty per cent – but it is still as loud a noise as anyone could possibly wish to endure. The saying will bring to mind a great deal of noise to any countryman.

Pyrrho's pig.

Said of a coward, after the Roman Pyrrho, who, it was claimed, remonstrated with panicking passengers on board a boat during a storm, pointing out that the pig being transported appeared totally unconcerned. Quoted by Montaigne in 1580.

The little pigs would grunt if they knew what the boar was suffering.

Scandinavian proverb dating back to AD 800.

Never ring a pig that has to root for a living.

Make sure you have the tools for the job; 20th century.

In times of adversity, the pig is called 'uncle'.

An Albanian saying, which reinforces the value of the pig to a peasant community in that when times get tough, it is more important than ever to look after your pig.

When the pig is proffered, open the bag.

Porcine equivalent to *caveat emptor* – let the buyer beware.

Every hog his own apple.

Be independent.

Pigs are the dirtiest of animals but the sweetest flesh.

'Old' Devon saying.

Drink soup with your wine or pay the Doctor with your swine.

Spanish admonishment not to drink on an empty stomach.

A pig rarely comes alone.

German proverb indicating that troubles infrequently arrive singly.

Never buy a pig from a miller or marry a girl from a pub!

Millers by reputation were not trusted, as it was thought that they short-changed their customers by keeping back a proportion of the milled grain, which probably is the origin of this saying. But why shouldn't you marry a girl from a pub?

Pigs born with black teeth never do well.

A practical saying relating to the fact that piglets inside the womb of a sow which are overdue, keep growing their teeth which sometimes become discoloured as well. Such litters are rarely good 'doers'.

As good to the purse is a sow as a cow.

The pig was always popular as the most prolific of farm stock.

He that can rear up a pig in his house
Hath cheaper his bacon and sweeter his souse.

Pigs provided almost the only meat that would over-winter.

It is hard to break a hog of an ill custom.

Equivalent to 'teaching an old dog new tricks'.

Make a hog or a dog of it.

Means to bring it to one use or another, with the implication, 'but make your mind up'.

With their snouts in the trough.

Of greed, especially political or corporate; 20th century.

There's more ways of killing pigs than choking them with butter.

Equivalent to 'there's more than one way to skin a cat'. Said to be of 19th century Shropshire origin.

A pig of my own sow.

Encouraging someone to help themselves from their own resources.

To run like a pig.

Very 20th century, as this relates to software that runs very slowly on given hardware.

To hog.

Another computer term, relating to the excessive amount of memory that a given piece of software occupies. Similarly used of human operators on shared systems, where it appears that ten per cent of the people use ninety per cent of the disk.

Beauty is in the sty of the beholder.

A 20th century aphorism. It was the winner of a competition to create a new piggy proverb organised by the Gloucestershire Old Spot Pig Breeders' Club, through the pages of *Country Living* magazine in 1994. Whilst to the unconverted pigs may be ugly, smelly, dirty or fat, to the man who owns a pig, nothing could be more appealing.

PIG'S FACE DAY

A religious festival is still celebrated in Gloucestershire every other year which has its origins in a love story from over 900 years ago. The event takes place in Avening, a small village between Tetbury and Nailsworth in the Cotswolds. (Some tourist guides say that the festival recalls the slaughter of a gigantic wild boar which ravaged crops there in times past – but this is a mundane explanation.)

Pig's Face Day actually relates to the tale of a lovelorn Queen Matilda. Before she married William the Conqueror, Matilda met and fell in love with Brittic, a Saxon lord, whilst he was on a mission to Flanders. However, her feelings were not reciprocated and he spurned her advances before returning to England. As every schoolboy knows, William duly conquered and the by now Queen Matilda travelled to England to be with her husband. On her arrival Matilda discovered that Brittic was residing at Avening Court, from whence she had him thrown into jail. There he died.

Matilda was overcome with remorse and, in his memory, had a church built in Avening. The building work was completed in 1080 and to celebrate she gave a feast for the builders which featured a boar's head, known colloquially as a pig's face.

Until as recently as the 1940s, Pig's Face Day was commemorated in September when all the village inns would serve pig's face sandwiches on the first Sunday after 14 September, Holy Cross Day. Around 1950, Canon Cuthbert Cooper reintroduced previous elements of the festival, with a boar's head being presented to one of the parishioners dressed as Queen Matilda, followed by a feast in the evening in the village hall. This modern adaptation is maintained to this day.

HOG THE HERO 2

The Saviour of Gloucester

Back to wartime for our next hero, who shares I suspect with all the others the fact that he was an unwitting 'volunteer'. This time, we go right back to the English Civil War of 1643. The action takes place in Gloucestershire. Already, Cirencester and Sudeley Castle have fallen to the Royalist Army, which has now marched on to the city of Gloucester itself and is encamped on Tredworth Field. A stalemate has arisen, with the highly fortified city holding out, against the odds, to an army of thirty thousand troops. The Royalists have become restless and frustrated and anxious to move on.

Inside the city walls, despite their brave resistance, the folk of Gloucester are becoming desperate. Having been cut off from the outside world for weeks by the siege, fresh food is becoming perilously scarce and it looks increasingly as if the attackers will win by starving the people into submission. Eventually, the situation reaches crisis point. There was only one live pig left in the whole city, all other livestock having been consumed. In one last effort, before the pig was killed, it was taken at dusk on to the city walls and encouraged, extremely roughly, to squeal like a banshee as it was paraded up and down.

Come daybreak, the populace of Gloucester were amazed to find that their enemy had decamped and left, apparently convinced that the city was brim-full of pigs and able to withstand the siege almost indefinitely. Nothing is recorded of the fate of that particular hero but one suspects that he may have provided a special feast for the celebrating chiefs of Gloucester.

To commemorate this hero pig, a ballad called *The Pig that Saved the City* was privately published in 1980, written by H. Y. J. Taylor and illustrated by Noreen Littleton. Here is a brief extract:

> We had one pig, and only one,
> No other pig to choose,
> We did the best which could be done
> To make that pig our ruse.

➤

From north to south, from east to west,
We marched that pig about
And with a pair of pinchers prest
Poor piggy in the snout.

Where'er he went his walks so wide,
He heard the poor pig crying,
And thought that dismal sound implied
A thousand pigs were dying.

That little pig which squealed with pain,
May well excite your pity,
And yet your gratitude must gain
For having saved your city.

The spy rushed back to Matson House,
And thus addressed his King,
'I crawled the ramparts like a mouse,
And doleful news I bring.'

A herd of Gloucestershire Old Spots.

THE DUNMOW FLITCH

This is the name of an ancient tradition, for which the prize was a flitch, or side, of bacon. It centres upon the village of Little Dunmow in Essex and goes back more than 800 years. The custom is said to have been started by a certain Lady Juga, who had founded the Priory of Dunmow in 1104, but it faded into oblivion until it was restored by Robert de Fitzwalter in 1244.

The prize was awarded to any couple who could kneel on the sharp stones by the Little Dunmow church door and swear the oath 'that he which repents him not of his marriage, either sleeping or waking, in a year and a day, may lawfully go to Dunmow and fetch a gammon of bacon'.

Chaucer mentions the practice in The Prologue to *The Wife of Bath's Tale*:

The bacoun was nought fet for hem, I trowe,
That som men feeche in Essex at Dunmowe.

Making the oath convincing was not easy, since between 1445 and 1772 there were only eight successful claimants:

1445 Richard Wright, labourer, Bawburgh, near Norwich.
1467 Steven Samuel, husbandman, Little Ayston, Essex.
1510 Thomas Ley, fuller, Coggeshall, Essex.
1701 William and Jane Parsley, butcher, Much Easton, Essex.
       John and Ann Reynolds, Hatfield Regis.
1751 Thomas Shakeshaft, woolcomber, Weathersfield, Essex.
1763 Names not recorded
1773 John and Susan Gilder, Tarling, Essex.

The 1751 ceremony was recorded in both *The Gentleman's Magazine* and *The London Magazine* and it was reported that the successful candidates earned a large sum of money by selling pieces of the Dunmow Flitch to members of the audience, who were said to number five thousand.

In 1778 a ballad opera written by Henry Bates was performed at the Haymarket Theatre in London. It included the following:

Ye good men and wives,
Who have lov'd all your lives
And whose vows have at no time been shaken,

➡

Now come and draw near,
With your conscience clear,
And demand a large flitch of Bacon.

Since a year and a day
Have in love roll'd away,
And an oath of that love has been taken,

On the sharp pointed stones,
With your bare marrow bones,
You have won our fam'd Priory Bacon.

The carved inn sign at the Flitch of
Bacon inn at Little Dunmow, Essex.

It is said that when Queen Victoria had been married for a year and a day,
the then Lord of the Manor at Dunmow privately offered a flitch of bacon
to Her Majesty but the gift was declined.

In 1851, a Mr and Mrs Hurrell, farmers from Felsted in Essex, laid claim
to the prize but the Lord of the Manor refused their claim stating that the
custom had been 'long dormant'. The local people, hearing this and fearing
that the custom would be abandoned, invited the couple to a presentation
of a flitch funded by local inhabitants at the fête at Easton Park near Dunmow on 16 July. There, having taken the customary oath, the Hurrells were
duly awarded their prize. Thereafter, the custom was revived again for
several decades.

A similar custom was noted at Tutbury in Staffordshire.

The plaque on the wall at the Flitch of Bacon.

Inn Signs

· THE BLUE BOAR ·

The name The Blue Boar goes back to the reign of King Richard III, he of hunchback and blackened character fame. Before being crowned, Richard was Duke of Gloucester and his arms included two white boars. His nickname, as Shakespeare recalls, was 'the Boar' (*see p.95*). Throughout history, publicans have been keen to show allegiance to the crown and many a tavern sported the sign of the white boar – until the Battle of Bosworth in 1485, that is. Nothing is likely to damage your trade more than maintaining loyalty to a defeated king and sign-writers of the time were kept busy, carefully over-painting all the white boars with blue paint. This was fortunately possible since one of those instrumental in Richard's downfall was the Earl of Oxford, whose cognisance was a blue boar! Most Blue Boars are depicted as being victorious on the cross of St George but there are exceptions to this rule. There are still many examples of pubs called The Blue Boar; and just to show that the exception proves the rule, there is at least one White Boar Hotel, at Bury in Lancashire.

This inn sign at Aldbourne in Wiltshire shows the traditional depiction of the victorious blue boar trampling on the king's colours.

Another traditional design at Longworth, Oxon.

Another famous Blue Boar was The George and Blue Boar which used to be located at 285 High Holborn in London. Its claim to fame was that it was the last house where the condemned would pause for a final drink on their way to Tyburn to be hanged.

'The Blue Pig' is a variation of The Blue Boar and the only example known is in Wolvey, Leicestershire. The inn was named The Blue Pig in 1800, before that having been known as The Blue Boar, The White Boar's Head and, originally, The Black Lion. *See also pages 72–74.* ➤→

A somewhat funkier version from Temple Grafton in Warwickshire.

THE BLUE (AND WHITE) BOAR – VARIATIONS ON A THEME...

A traditional Blue Boar at Chipping Norton in Oxfordshire.

The only White Boar at Bury in Lancashire.

➤➤

The Blue Pig, depicting a Middle White at Wolvey, Leicestershire.

An exotic portrayal of a blue boar at The Blue Boar Inn at Hermitage in Berkshire.

The Blue Boar in Ludlow, where the signwriter seems to have run short of blue paint.

A heraldic-style Blue Boar in Abingdon, Oxfordshire.

The Blue Boar Hotel in Maldon, Essex, the boar with a Mohican mane.

Sow and boar depicted in a woodcut from the Renaissance.

· THE WILD BOAR ·

The Wild Boar is less a heraldic symbol than a statement of local history. Most inns so named are in areas where boars were once hunted. For instance, in the case of The Wild Boar Hotel at Crook, Windermere, there is a legend that the last boar in Westmorland was killed outside it, a story which dates back to the 16th century. Other examples of the Wild Boar exist at Congleton, Staffordshire, and at Wincle, Macclesfield, although the latter only received its name in the last forty years or so. There is an instance of a Boar Inn at Moddershall, near Stone in Staffordshire. The boar was also the emblem of the Roman legion that helped to build Hadrian's Wall and a stone carving of the beast was found at Corbridge in Northumberland.

The Wild Boar at Crook has this statue in the grounds, said to be the burial place of the last wild boar in Westmorland.

'AS DRUNK AS DAVY'S SOW'

David Lloyd was a Welshman who kept an alehouse at Hereford in about 1670. In the pigsty at the back he kept a freak sow which had been born with six legs. This animal was part of the attraction of the inn and people from miles around would visit the place to see the sow, which was doubtless good for business. One day Mrs Lloyd, suffering from the effects of over-indulgence, lay down in the straw in the sty to sleep it off. Her husband, not aware of her plight, brought round a group of visitors and on approaching the sty, proudly proclaimed, 'There is a sow for you! Did you ever see the like?' which brought the response from one of the sightseers, 'Well, it is the drunkenest sow I ever beheld!' From that day on, his wife was known as 'Davy's Sow'.

· THE BUTCHERS ARMS ·

Doubtless, many Butchers Arms up and down the country include on the signboard some representation of a pig but just one in particular is exceptional. The pub is located at Sheepscombe, high on the Cotswolds between Stroud and Gloucester. Above the painted sign is a splendid carving depicting the butcher, wearing his striped apron and sitting on his stool. In his right hand is a tankard of foaming ale. At his feet, a pig is struggling to escape, but the rope securing its hind leg is tangled around the butcher's ankles. The dilemma facing the butcher is whether to lose his pig or his pint!

The Butchers Arms, Sheepscombe, between Stroud and Gloucester.

· THE SOW AND PIGS ·

The most famous of such hostelries is that at Toddington in Bedfordshire. The origin of the name is obscure although it is most likely to indicate 'a house of plenty' as the pig and her litter have always been associated with good living. Alternatively, the name may have derived from a game of cards called 'My Sow's Pigg'd', said to have been popular among farmers between the 17th and 19th centuries. In recent times, the Bedfordshire pub has had a resident poet, Alan Harris, who penned, among others, the following lines:

The Sow and Pigs has a sort of treaty
To preserve a bench for Flo and Beattie,
And should unwitting strangers steal their places
See the disbelief on Flo's and Beattie's faces.

Other Sow and Pigs pubs include those in: Culham, Abingdon, Oxford-shire; Hill Top, West Bromwich; Irthlingborough, Northamptonshire; and Thundridge, Hertfordshire.

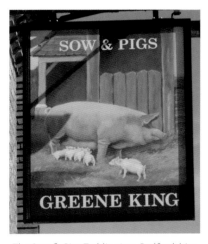

The Sow & Pigs, Toddington, Bedfordshire.   *The Sow & Pigs, Thundridge, Herts.*

The Sow & Pigs, Poundon, Oxon.

· THE HOG IN THE POUND ·

Otherwise known as 'the gentleman in trouble'. This ancient inn in Oxford Street, London, still stands and is famous for the bloody exploits of its one-time landlady, Catherine Hayes. Having taken in a lover, she was persuaded by him to do away with her husband, which she did by cutting off his head, placing it in a bag and throwing it in the Thames. But the bag came ashore at low tide and when the head was found it was placed on a pole in St Margaret's Churchyard, Westminster, so that it might be identified – which it duly was. The lover was hanged and Catherine Hayes was burnt alive at Tyburn in 1726. The tavern took its name from the earlier use of the premises as a butcher's shop. Then, its sign was a pig in a sty and the visual pun was maintained with its change of use. A 'Pig in the Pound' exists at Romford.

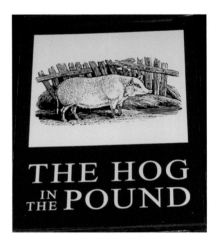

The Hog in the Pound, Oxford Street, London.

· THE BOAR'S HEAD ·

Another frequently found name for a pub or hotel. The reasons for the name can vary from place to place but most likely concerns the tradition of Queen's College, Oxford, of serving a boar's head as the main feast at Christmas – a tradition well recorded to this day in 'The Boar's Head Carol'. Such an association would have implied the very best in eating, drinking and merrymaking.

An alternative origin may be the association with some local aristocracy, such as the Gordon family, whose coat of arms included a heraldic boar's head. (Gordon's gin still sports this symbol as a trade mark on the label of the famous green bottle.) In addition, at one time the privilege of licensing alehouses fell to the De Warenne family, the Earls of Surrey, and the name may have been taken from one of their crests as a not very subtle way of trying to influence their judgement in granting a licence. At Perry Barr, Birmingham, the boar's head is shown as part of a totem pole and relates to the arms of the local Gough family.

Whatever the origins, one of the most famous inns of all times was known as The Boar's Head and stood at Eastcheap in London for many centuries. Made famous by the exploits of Falstaff, as recorded by Shakespeare, the inn actually existed and the first recorded evidence dates back to the reign of Richard II in the late 1300s. Later, its sign was inscribed, 'This is the chief tavern in London'. It became the logical meeting place for the annual Shakespearean dinner party, the last of which was held in 1784 and included among its notable guests the politicians Wilberforce and Pitt. The original inn was destroyed by the Great Fire but was rebuilt on the same site. In 1831 it was demolished to make way for road building for the approaches to London Bridge.

The Boar's Head at Ardington near Wantage, Oxfordshire, one of the loveliest inn signs anywhere.

One story associated with The Boar's Head at Eastcheap took place in May 1718 when James Austin, 'inventor of the Persian ink powder', wishing to give his customers a feast to remember as 'substantial proof of his gratitude', commissioned the making of a giant plum pudding to be served at The Boar's Head. The pudding weighed 1,000lbs and was put in the copper at The Red Lion inn in Southwark on Monday, 12 May and boiled for

The Boars Head at Standish near Wigan in Lancashire.

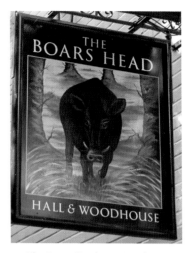

The Boars Head near Horsham, West Sussex.

fourteen days. From there it was transported to The Swan tavern in Fish Street Hill accompanied by a band playing, 'What lumps of pudding my mother gave me'. The transport was provided by six asses, as the pudding was 18 feet 2 inches long and 4 feet in diameter. However, before the journey was completed and The Boar's Head reached, the smell was apparently too much for the watching crowds and the pudding was hijacked and devoured. (And we think that PR is a modern phenomenon!)

The Boars Head at Hampton Lucy in Warwickshire shows Falstaff outside the famous inn referred to by Shakespeare.

· THE DOG AND BACON ·

This pub at Horsham in Sussex is so named as a corruption of the 'Dorking Beacon' (reputedly a bonfire on Horsham Common nearby), which could be seen from the pub.

Dog & Bacon, Horsham, West Sussex.

THE BREWERY PIG

In many ways, pigs and pubs are synonymous. Pigs were (and in certain instances, still are), kept at breweries to convert spoiled beer and the brewer's grain, left over after the malting process, into saleable protein. In the 1980s Adnams in Suffolk found that they could significantly cut their charges from the local water board for the disposal of waste by feeding it to pigs instead of flushing it down the drain. There are many recorded instances of pigs getting drunk on such feed and suffering the inevitable after-effects as well. Sadly, the recession in farming meant that in 2001 the Adnams pigs were sold and the waste materials converted into fertiliser instead. The Kent brewer, Shepherd Neame, ran a similar scheme but had to cut the daily intake from eight pints to six per pig in 1981 as the brewery pigs were showing signs of inebriation on the higher ration.

· THE GOLDEN BOAR ·

This may refer to a local heraldic boar as it is found at just one pub at Frekenham, Cambridgeshire, close to the Suffolk border. Alternatively, it may have some obscure reference to ancient Scandinavian mythology since the golden boar, *Gullinbursti* (Golden Bristles), was the one upon which the god Freyr rode and which drew his chariot. The boar was faster through air and water than any horse and the reflected glow from his golden coat meant that he created sufficient light wherever he went.

The Golden Boar, Frekenham, Cambridgeshire

· THE GLOUCESTER OLD SPOT ·

This inn is at Piffs Elm, between Cheltenham and Tewkesbury in Gloucestershire, and its name celebrates the fine local breed of pig. Unfortunately it too received this name only comparatively recently so there is no significant tale to tell about the naming after the county hero.

· THE OLD SPOT ·

The Old Spot is the second inn in Gloucestershire named after the county's pig and is located in Dursley.

The pub is a favourite of real ale fans and was declared the CAMRA (Campaign for Real Ale) Pub of the Year in 2008. Among the ales on offer is the locally-produced range from Uley Brewery, which includes Old Spot Ale.

The Gloucester Old Spot at Piffs Elm, between Cheltenham and Tewkesbury in Gloucestershire.

Logo of the Uley Brewery.

The Old Spot, Dursley, Gloucestershire.

· HOGSHEAD ·

This name refers to a barrel of 52 or 54 gallons capacity, which, traditionally, the apprentice had to make as his final task. It is now widely used as a name for a pub that has little or no historical connection with that tradition.

Those in Newbury, Berkshire, and Hove, East Sussex, are illustrated.

The Hog's Head, Newbury, Berkshire.

The Hogshead, Hove, East Sussex.

· THE THREE PIGS, THE TWO PIGS, THE LITTLE PIG ·

These are mostly modern pub names given without historical reference. The Three Pigs at Edgefield, Norfolk, was formerly 'The Bacon Arms' but Lord Bacon refused permission to allow his coat of arms to be used on the sign and the name was thus changed in 1976. One other instance of a name change that did not take place was at The Nag's Head in Oxford, once frequented by Evelyn Waugh. The brewers, Ind Coope, apparently wanted to change the name to The Pig and Truffle but there was no historical precedent. The locals objected to any change, and they won. The Little Pig at Amblecote may have more to do with the local glass-making industry than agriculture. The sign is said to represent a 'sow and six', a glass ornament.

The Two Pigs near Corsham in Wiltshire.

NOTED FOR SUPPING ALE

There is a memorial stone on the forecourt of The Cock Hotel, Worsley, Lancashire, to a pig noted for supping ale. 'In memory of Polly, mother of 200 piglets died Dec. 3rd 1904, aged 15 years.'

· THE PIG AND WHISTLE ·

Although not widespread in its current use as a pub name, this must be one of the best-known titles in the trade. The reasons behind the combination are obscure and many theories exist. Rather than champion any particular one, the various ideas are listed here for you to select which you think best applies:

1 The concept of a pig and whistle is ancient and is seen represented in carvings in churches including Winchester Cathedral. They were also widely used in illustrated manuscripts. The name, therefore, may simply have been adopted from these illustrations.

2 It may be a corruption of the Saxon, *piggen*, a milking pail, and *wassail*, to be in good health. In the early history of alehouses, beer was served in pails and the customers would dip their vessels into the bucket and serve themselves. Thus, a Pig and Whistle, providing the play on words was readily understood, was a place where the ale was plentiful and the customers could expect to be in good heart.

3 The next suggestion goes back to Danish-Saxon, in which the term *pige-washail* was the Angel's Salutation to the Virgin Mary and meant 'Health to the Maiden'.

4 The 'pig' was supposed to relate to the Anglo-Saxon practice, made lawful by King Edgar, of marking drinking vessels with 'pegs' to indicate how much had been consumed. Each guest drank down to the next peg and such practices gave rise to the expression, 'to take someone down a peg or two', originally a reference to sharing in hospitality. The 'whistle' again refers to *wassail* and a general feeling of Bacchanalian good cheer. Once again, this explanation demands that the verbal puns are widely understood or the purpose is surely lost. A 'Peg and Whistle' does exist at Helions Bumpstead in Essex.

> Come, old fellow, drink down to your peg!
> But do not drink any further, I beg!
> – Longfellow [*Christus. The Golden Legend.* Pt IV]

5 A variation of the above suggests that the 'pig' refers to the Anglo-Saxon word for a meeting place, *pightle*.

The Pig & Whistle, Stotfold, Hertfordshire.   *The Pig & Whistle, Bridgewater, Somerset.*

6 Scotland provides two possible explanations. The first is a play on *Pyx and Housel*, Scottish for 'a pot and small change'. This theory is backed up by the expression 'to go to pigs and whistles', which has the same meaning as 'to go to pot'.

7 The second Scottish offering concerns the superstitions of fisherman and sailors. In Scotland especially, it is taboo to use the word 'pig' on board ship and other words would be used such as 'old grumphie' or 'the beast' should it become necessary to mention the creature. It is also extremely unlucky to whistle on board ship since this calls up the winds and will result in storms. Thus, this theory has it that, once safely on shore, the sailor could return to such practices with a clear conscience and the local inn was then a symbol of this. Were all 'Pigs and Whistles' sited along the northern coasts, then one might give more credence to this theory – but the few who have adopted the title in recent history are not so situated.

8 It is believed in certain quarters that 'pig and whistle' is a visual play on that other popular sign, the 'bear and ragged staff' (used for example, by Warwickshire County Council as their logo). This theory works on the basis that, at some stage, a poorly painted bear and ragged staff was derisively referred to as more like a pig and whistle and the name stuck.

The Pig & Whistle, Totnes, Devon.

In much the same way, 'The Elephant and Castle' in London has long been known colloquially as 'The Pig and Tinderbox'.

Whichever explanation you choose, there is one pub in Redcar which adopted this name as recently as 1977 for the very best of logical reasons. It was previously known as The Alexandra. John Smith's Tadcaster Brewery explain the story thus:

> Before the main railway station was built at Redcar, ironstone was loaded into railway wagons in the marshalling yard behind The Alexandra for distribution further north. The Alexandra was also near a pig slaughterhouse which employed approximately 60 people. Being a small pub, The Alexandra could not accommodate the workers from the marshalling yard and the workers from the slaughter-house. The men from the slaughterhouse frequented The Alexandra between 11.30am and 12 noon. At 12 noon the engine men used to blow a whistle to let the customers in the pub know that they were on their way – the pig men left and the pub was used for a further half an hour by the rail men. This whistle became known as the 'pig whistle' and the pub by the same name.

In a slightly similar way, there was a Pig and Whistle pub in Liverpool where Irish drovers would drink whilst awaiting the train on which they were to load their charges. As soon as the train was ready, the driver would blow his whistle, a sign for drinking up and the departure of the Irishmen to load their pigs on board. In Edinburgh, there is an inn whose name plays on this title, known as The Pig and Thistle.

· THE JOLLY FARMER ·

The Jolly Farmer (a distinct rarity in this day and age) still exists with the same sign at Bramley near Guildford in Surrey although the Watneys brand above the cheerful fellow has long since disappeared as an embarrassing reminder of the hideous chemical beers of the 1960s.

The pig upon which he rides is quite jolly too!

· THE FARMERS ARMS ·

This Farmers Arms is located in the village of Apperley near Gloucester and whilst genuine farmers might complain about the depiction of the agriculturalist in this scene, it does at least include an example of our hero.

The Jolly Farmer, Bramley, near Guildford, Surrey.

The Farmers Arms, Apperley, near Gloucester.

KARAOKE BROADWAY-STYLE

Pigs, for all their associations with pubs and therefore alcohol, are generally not expected to be found on licensed premises, except in the ways described elsewhere, but that wasn't always the case. We tend to think of (mainly) inebriated people standing up and singing in a pub as a recent phenomenon invented by the Japanese but it seems that karaoke goes back to earlier times, at least in the town of Broadway in the Cotswolds. Early in the last century, it was apparently the custom for pub-goers to stand up and sing but with one small encumbrance – a live suckling pig under one arm. The pig wriggled, the pig squealed and the audience laughed and heckled and between man and beast did everything possible to put off the performer. Once he lost his way or broke down in laughter, he had lost the contest and it was another's turn. (I blame tourism myself – one Oriental visitor must have spied this local custom and taken it back to Tokyo or wherever, and now you hardly ever see a pig in a pub but karaoke machines are everywhere…)

SOW STATUESQUE!

In England, the town of Calne in Wiltshire was once dominated by the Harris's Bacon Factory, the major employer and benefactor of the town for decades. The civic authority struck a bronze of two resting pigs in recognition of that relationship. Alas, the bacon factory is no more and the only reminder today is those two bronze pigs in the shopping arcade.

The bronze pigs at Calne.

MR PROLIFIC

Pigs are the smallest of all mammals when they are born, in relation to their eventual size and weight. This means that they grow faster and more efficiently than other species. At the time of birth, they are 1/300th of their adult body weight, whilst humans are roughly 1/20th and rats and elephants approximately 1/40th. That gives the pig a rate of growth far greater than all other meat providers and makes him especially useful to the human diet. Their efficiency in food conversion is also superior to other farm stock; pigs will convert three pounds of grain into a pound of flesh whereas cattle and sheep require nearly 10 pounds of cereal fodder to achieve the same result.

The pig is also a prolific breeder, at a maximum rate of two-and-a-half litters a year, the largest recorded of which was 37 pigs born. Compare that with cattle, who raise at most two calves a year, with sheep struggling to produce four lambs in the same period. Part of the reason for this can be found in the following: the boar will produce 150–250cc of ejaculate compared with just 1cc for a ram, 3–5cc for a bull and 70–100cc for a stallion. Whilst the concentration of sperm is not as high for pigs as for other animals, the extra volume ensures that the number of sperm per ejaculate is 25–50 billion, a number which maintains the high fertility rate of the pig. The stallion is next at 7–10 billion, the bull 3–5 billion and the poor old ram just 1 billion. It's surprising that sheep exist at all!

The pig is by far the most efficient and prolific farm animal.

Large Blacks at Duchy Home Farm, Tetbury.

The Gloucestershire Old Spots or Orchard Pig, the oldest pedigree spotted pig in the world. Local folklore says that the spots on this breed are bruises from windfall fruit.

HELPING THE WAR EFFORT

Of course, World War I began in 1914 and a Gloucestershire Old Spots boar almost spiked the Kaiser's guns before it all started. The spotted pig from the West Country was at its most popular during this period up to the mid-1920s and caught the eye of the Kaiser, who was something of a pig fancier himself. He had asked the GOS Society's Secretary, Eldred G. Walker, to select him a prime boar for shipment to Germany, the breed's first official export, and Mr Walker had duly toured the South West in pursuit of the best example he could find. The deal had been done and the cheque in full settlement received, when, just a few hours before war was officially declared, the Kaiser sent a cable which read: 'DON'T SHIP PIG UNTIL FURTHER ORDERS'. The cheque was banked but the boar was never sent, so the Gloucestershire Old Spots did their bit towards depleting the Kaiser's war chest.

Winterbourne Blanco was a champion Gloucestershire Old Spots in 1920 and depicts the type of pig that caught the Kaiser's eye.

A propaganda postcard from World War I issued to Allied servicemen to send home.

TESTING THE ATOM BOMB

Another similarity between man and pig is the effect of radiation on our bodies. During atom-bomb tests on the Bikini atoll in 1946, a pig (Pig 311), was among 3,352 animals placed close to the detonation site. After the explosion, she was spotted swimming calmly in the sea. She grew into a 600lb sow and went to live at Washington's Zoological Park, showing no ill-effects other than that she proved to be sterile.

Pigs In Shakespeare

SHYLOCK: Some men there are love not a gaping pig;
    Some, that are mad if they behold a cat;
    And others, when the bagpipe sings i' the nose,
    Cannot contain their urine...
    And there is no firm reason to be render'd,
    Why he cannot abide a gaping pig;
    Why he, a harmless necessary cat;
    Why he, a woollen bag-pipe; but of force
    Must yield to such inevitable shame
    As to offend, himself being offended;
    So can I give no reason, nor will I not,
    More than a lodged hate, and a certain loathing
    I bear Antonio, that I follow thus
    A losing suit against him.
    – *The Merchant of Venice*, Act IV, sc. i

LEAR: What hast thou been?

EDGAR: A serving-man, proud in heart and mind; that curled my hair; wore gloves in my cap; served the lust of my mistress' heart, and did the act of darkness with her; swore as many oaths as I spake words, and broke them in the sweet face of heaven: one that slept in the contriving of lust, and waked to do it: wine loved I deeply, dice dearly; and in woman out-paramoured the Turk: false of heart, light of ear, bloody of hand; hog in sloth, fox in stealth, wolf in greediness, dog in madness, lion in prey.
    – *King Lear*, Act III, sc. iv

DOLL TEARSHEET: Thou whoreson little tidy Bartholomew boar-pig, when wilt thou leave fighting o' days and foining o' nights, and begin to patch up thine old body for heaven?
– *The Merry Wives of Windsor*, Act III, sc. iv

FLUELLEN: What call you the town's name where Alexander the Pig was born?'

GOWER: Alexander the Great.

FLUELLEN: Why, I pray you, is not pig great?
The pig, or the great, or the mighty, or the huge,
or the magnanimous, are all one reckonings,
save the phrase is a little variations.
– *Henry V,* Act IV, sc. vii

SHYLOCK: Yes, to smell pork; to eat of the habitation which your prophet the Nazarite conjured the devil into. I will buy with you, sell with you, talk with you, walk with you and so following; but I will not eat with you, nor pray with you.
– *The Merchant of Venice*, Act I, sc. iii

DROMIO: The capon burns, the pig falls from the spit,
the clock hath strucken twelve.
– *The Comedy of Errors*, Act I, sc. ii

RICHMOND: The Wretched, bloody and usurping boar,
That spoiled your summer fields and fruitful vines,
… this foul swine,
Lies now even in the centre of this isle,
Near to the town of Leicester, as we learn.
– *Richard III, Act V,* sc. ii

FALSTAFF: I do walk here before thee like a sow that hath overwhelmed all her litter but one.
 – *King Henry IV, Part II*, Act I, sc. ii

PETRUCHIO: Think you a little din can daunt mine ears?
Have I not in my time heard lions roar?
Have not heard the sea puff'd up with winds
Rage like an angry boar chafed with sweat?
 – *The Taming of the Shrew*, Act I, sc. ii

JESSICA: In converting Jews to Christians, you raise the price of pork.
 – *The Merchant of Venice*, Act III, sc. v

FALSTAFF: On, bacons, on!
 – *Henry IV Part I*, Act II, sc. ii

AARON: Weke, weke! So cries a pig prepared to the spit.
 – *Titus Andronicus,* Act IV, sc. ii

HASTINGS: To fly the boar before the boar pursues,
Were to incense the boar to follow us
And make pursuit where he did mean no chase.
 – *Richard III,* Act III, sc. ii

FALSTAFF: …prodigals lately come from swine-keeping…
 – *Henry IV, Part I*, Act IV, sc. ii

MERCUTIO: O, then, I see Queen Mab hath been with you...
And sometime comes she with a tithe-pig's tail
Tickling a parson's nose as a' lies asleep,
The dreams he of another benefice.
– *Romeo and Juliet*, Act I, sc. iv

ORLANDO: Shall I keep your hogs and eat husks with them?
What prodigal position have I spent, that I should come to such penury?
– *As You Like It*, Act I, sc. i

SHEEP PIGS

It seems that whatever a dog can do, a pig can do... as well. In 1889, there appeared in a journal called *The Zoologist* a report from a Mr F. V. Darbyshire, of Balliol College, Oxford.

He had been staying at Gavinana near Pistoia in Italy. There, he reported, the peasants dwelling in the Apennines had large tracts of chestnut forest and many of them kept flocks of sheep. However, being poor, they could not afford sheep dogs and thus had trained the local variety of mountain pigs, a small breed, to aid them with their flocks. The pigs were very effective, as clever as dogs, and kept the sheep together and prevented them from straying.

In the last few years, a similar example has occurred in Wales, except that this time the pigs just about trained themselves! Clive and Ian Watters ran the Gower Farm Museum in South Wales and had three little pigs that followed them round the farm – one Tamworth and two wild boar. The pigs started to imitate the sheep dogs and were soon rounding up the sheep in just the same way. Taken in hand, the pigs would react to instructions given by the brothers and were as effective as any dogs. The brothers sold the farm and took the two wild boar with them but the Tamworth stayed at the museum, earning his keep by rounding up the sheep.

The idea of a sheep-pig was used, of course, by the makers of the 1995 film *Babe*, based on a children's story by Dick King-Smith, *The Sheep-Pig*. But, as we see above, truth is often stranger than fiction.

THE CHINESE HOROSCOPE

The Chinese do not follow the system of the twelve signs of the Zodiac that is found in the Western world. Their system contains twelve different animals, representing different years. So instead of Libra, Virgo and Pisces, for example, the Chinese celebrate the Year of... the Rat, the Ox, the Tiger and the Snake, among others. By now, you will not be surprised to learn that one of those others is our friend the Pig, but his inclusion, according to folklore, owes something to the devious rat.

The Jade King resided in Heaven and ruled Earth but had never actually visited Earth and so knew little of it. Having his every need met by aides and servants, he was bored, so called his chief adviser to him and asked him what the animals on Earth looked like. The adviser told him that there were many creatures on Earth and asked the King if he wished to see them all.

'Oh no!' replied the King. 'I shall waste too much time if I do that. Instead I want you to select the twelve most interesting animals, and I will grade them according to their peculiarity.'

The adviser thought long and hard about which animals to present to the King. His first choice was the rat and he asked the rat to pass on an invitation to his friend the cat. Other invitations went out to the ox, the tiger, the dragon, the rabbit, the snake, the monkey, the horse, the ram, the dog and the rooster and all were expected to attend the palace at six o'clock next morning.

The rat duly informed the cat but the cat was afraid he would oversleep and asked the rat to wake him in good time to make his appointment at the palace. But as the night wore on, the rat thought about the next morning. He was very proud to be invited to attend the Jade King but was afraid that he, an ugly rat, would be upstaged by his beautiful friend the cat, and so he let him sleep on while he quietly slipped away to the palace.

The animals were duly lined up for inspection and the Jade King walked along the line admiring each one. But when he reached the end, he turned to his adviser and said, 'They are all very interesting, but why are there only eleven?'

The adviser had no answer and in fear that the King might be angry at his incompetence, sent a servant down to Earth to bring back the first

➥

animal he could find. The servant arrived on a road to find a man with a pig, so he took the pig and carried it back to join the parade.

In the meantime, the rat was afraid that he would not stand out among such large animals, so he jumped on the back of the ox and played the flute. The King was delighted and made him number one among animals, and the ox, for his kindness towards the rat, number two. Third was the tiger because he looked so courageous and the rabbit was fourth on account of his fine white fur. The dragon was deemed to look like a strong snake on legs and was placed fifth and the snake itself came sixth. The horse was seventh, the ram eighth, the monkey ninth, the rooster tenth and the dog eleventh. All that was left was the pig, which the Jade King thought was ugly but it was the only animal left and so it was designated the twelfth.

After the ceremony was over, the cat finally arrived and begged the King to place him but the King said he could not because all the places had been allocated. The cat spotted the rat and chased him, and the Chinese believe that the rat's deception led to the cat never again being able to tolerate the rat in his presence.

The Year of the Pig falls in 1911, 1923, 1935, 1947, 1959, 1971, 1983, 1995, 2007 and 2019. People born under that sign are said to be honest, tolerant, generous and profoundly self-centred. However, there are far more complicated predictions to be made than these and a whole science, every bit as complicated as that for horoscopes, exists for further study.

Among famous 'pigs' are Julie Andrews, Maria Callas, Oliver Cromwell, Henry VIII, Ernest Hemingway, Alfred Hitchcock, Albert Schweitzer, both Fred Astaire and Ginger Rogers, Humphrey Bogart, Ronald Reagan, Noël Coward, Sir Elton John, Woody Allen, Sarah Duchess of York and David Essex.

Piggy People

∞

MANY FAMOUS PEOPLE HAVE been associated with pigs throughout history, which is not surprising given the importance of these animals, as we have seen. In modern times, too, many well-known people have had an association with the porker, usually in the form of keeping them. Thus we can say that John the Baptist, Winston Churchill, James Dean, Queen Mary and Lord Runcie all had pigs in common.

Some people collect model pigs, in china, glass, wood, fabric or even plastic. The Duke of Edinburgh, for example, is said to have a fine collection, mostly of china, whilst the American tennis player, Gigi Fernandez, is reputed to have around 170 items in her collection but has of course been collecting for less time. In 1995 at Wimbledon, Gigi wore shorts decorated with four pink pigs with 'cheerfully knotted tails'. (Prince Philip has not been reported as appearing in public wearing any of his collection.)

Many people are enthusiastic collectors of pig-related paraphernalia, as the number of items in the high street or for sale at any time on Ebay confirms. Obviously they share their hobby with some exalted company.

From those who collect china pigs to those who collect Chinese (oriental) pigs… The fashion for keeping pigs as pets seems to have arisen largely in the USA, once Vietnamese Pot Bellies became established there. Among notable devotees have been Ian Botham, the former England cricketer, whose pig is called Baldric; and John Francome, the television racing presenter and former National Hunt jockey, whose pet was a black VPB called Candy. Leading Flat trainer Ian Balding bought his wife a pet Vietnamese pig as a present. Motorcycle racer Carl Fogarty had two VPBs, named after his two leading rivals. Former footballer and now actor Vinnie Jones claims to have several of them. Fellow Hollywood star George Clooney also had a VPB pet, called Max. Pop star Belinda Carlisle also once had a VPB as a pet but found him to be just too much of a handful. Television chef and restaurateur Antony Worrall Thompson also had VPBs but has since become a keeper of Middle Whites.

More recently, former Spice Girl Victoria Beckham bought a miniature pig as a present for her husband, David. Luckily their home is roomy, as rumour has it that these latest mini-pigs don't stay small for long. Television and radio personality Jonathan Ross also keeps two as pets.

Collectable pigs come in many forms.

Another pig story was associated with a cricketer during the 1982–83 Ashes tour of Australia. Mike Gatting, noted for his successful English captaincy against the Australians, was also renowned for his healthy appetite and a matching girth. During one Test match, play was interrupted when a rotund piglet with the word 'GATT' painted on its side was released on to the field of play!

Not a Vietnamese Pot Belly but a wild boar was the childhood pet of actor Martin Wenner as he grew up in Bolivia. Called *Dona Pancha*, she was acquired as a piglet from an old lady who lived on the edge of the jungle. The wild boar grew quickly but remained tame and friendly. Martin recalls that she could consume plums with the speed of a conveyor belt, shovelling them through one side of her mouth whilst ejecting the stones equally quickly from the other.

The famous 19th century landscape gardener, Gertrude Jekyll, was much too practical a person to keep a pig as a pet. Instead, she kept pigs for a very good reason – to supply her with high quality manure.

SIR WINSTON CHURCHILL kept his own pigs at Chartwell. He also loved cars, and had close contact with Lord Rootes. (Rootes Motors made marques including Hillman, Singer, Humber and Sunbeam.) One day,

Rootes, driving a prototype Humber estate car, turned up at Chartwell to buy some pigs. The car caught the politician's eye and he demanded to be able to have it for his planned painting holiday. Although the motor magnate protested, Churchill was adamant – 'no car, no pigs' – until he got his way. Lord Rootes was seen to leave in another vehicle, well loaded up with bartered pigs from the Churchill breeding stock.

Sir Winston was again associated with pigs in 1954 after the release of the cartoon film of *Animal Farm*. Labour MP Herbert Morrison raised the question in Parliament as to why he had allowed his likeness to be used to portray one of the pig characters in the film, Old Major. Before any reply could be made, the Speaker demanded that the question be withdrawn, which Morrison reluctantly did. One of the animators, John Halas, admitted later that the Old Major character had indeed been based on the great man, but he was amazed that anyone had noticed.

THOSE WHO KEEP PIGS on their land because they like having them around include the Prince of Wales and the Princess Royal, both of whom keep small numbers of Large Blacks and Tamworths, and Gloucestershire Old Spots, at Highgrove and Gatcombe Park respectively. The Duchess of Devonshire also has a GOS sow at Chatsworth. Tamworths reside at Lord Lichfield's Shugborough Estate at Stafford. Lord Salisbury – the politician who fell on his sword as Conservative leader in the House of Lords after secret dealings with Tony Blair – breeds Tamworth and Large Black pigs on his Dorset estate. The former Archbishop of Canterbury, Lord Runcie, mentioned above, has long kept Berkshire pigs in Kent and one of his illustrious predecessors, Thomas à Becket, also kept pigs. A Lord Hartington of the Victorian era (1833–1908) might well have been the model for P. G. Wodehouse's porcine-loving Lord Emsworth. Sitting in the House of Lords, a fellow peer during a speech was heard to claim that this was the proudest moment of his life. Turning to his neighbour, Hartington commented, 'The proudest moment of my life was when my pig won the first prize at Skipton Fair!'

Meanwhile over in the Commons, a one-time junior agriculture minister in John Major's government (up to 1997) was Tony Baldry, a relative rarity amongst sitting MPs as he had his own Gloucestershire Old Spots.

Some of the Prince of Wales's organic Tamworth pigs at Duchy Home Farm, adjacent to Highgrove.

OTHER NOTABLES INVOLVED in pig keeping include Queen Mary. She spent much of the duration of World War II at Badminton, home of the Duke of Beaufort, where she enthusiastically did her bit for the war effort by adopting a Saddleback pig to consume the household waste, as people were exhorted to do in wartime Britain. Sir Walter Scott also kept pigs as did the singer James Taylor, and the publisher and novelist Michael Korda. So too did Beatrix Potter, at her farm in the Lake District. Among current keepers of Gloucestershire Old Spots are Blur bassist, now columnist, Alex James, and actress and model Liz Hurley. Those who favour British Saddlebacks include former Formula One champion Jody Scheckter and television star Jimmy Doherty.

The late actor James Dean had been brought up on a farm and looked after the pigs before going into the world of films. Another actor, James Purefoy, had a job as a pig castrator before going into films. On a good day, he reckoned to deprive up to fifty of the little porkers of their boar-hood. Eric Robson, chairman of BBC Radio 4's *Gardeners' Question Time*, keeps Tamworth pigs on his smallholding in Cumbria and writer and broadcaster Paul Heiney had Large Blacks on his Suffolk farm. Jenni Murray, who presents *Woman's Hour* on Radio 4, has a smallholding in Cheshire where she breeds pigs among other animals. That witty artist, Beryl Cook, has also kept pigs, which perhaps accounts for the number which appear in her works.

The late, popular radio DJ and television broadcaster, John Peel, often referred to his wife, Sheila, by her affectionate nickname of 'Pig'. Janis Joplin, pop icon of the 1960s, also bore that nickname although not always as affectionately.

A PIG ONCE OCCUPIED the White House. Theodore Roosevelt was the president at the time and his son, Quentin, was a keen collector of pets. On a trip to Virginia he acquired a small piglet for a dollar and took it back to his illustrious home. After twenty-four hours, his mother put her foot down and demanded its removal. He took it to the well-known Washington pet shop, Schmid's Emporium of Pets, and sold it to Mr Schmid for $1.25, thus showing a keen business sense. Equal to the challenge, the store owner placed the pig in the window under a sign 'This pig slept in the White House last night. Price $3.50' and sold it within hours! Mr Schmid proudly displayed on the wall a framed letter from Theodore Roosevelt reading: 'I shall never forget how all the boys, and especially Quentin, used to enjoy your store.'

The Vietnamese Pot Belly has played its part in fund-raising, too, and features in a world record. In 1991, two radio production assistants kissed two Vietnamese, originally named Pinky and Perky, 3,001 times in one hour. At least now no one can call them faint-hearted!

Vietnamese Pot Belly piglets.

Probably the most eccentric pig keeper was Lord Gardenstone, a Scottish judge who died in 1793. His favourite pig literally shared his life with him, sitting at table and dining with his master. He accompanied him to church where he sat in a special pew and slept in the judge's bedroom on a pile of his clothes, specially laid out for His Porkship.

Pet pigs are not always welcome away from their homes. It was reported in 1992 that a Devon landlady had banned a pet pig from her pub after it made unwelcome advances towards women customers after imbibing. Dorothy Lomas, landlady of the Atmospheric Railway Inn at Starcross said: 'He would have a couple too many and start snuffling around women's ankles.'

Wild boar have even been treated as pets, although it is doubtful if British officialdom would be as accommodating as their French counterparts. In the South of France, a farmer, Louis Evesque, kept and reared a wild boar piglet, known affectionately as Chirac. Claimed to be entirely tame, the animal would walk to heel and beg on its hind-legs. After it reached the age of ten months, the authorities got to hear of it and ordered its destruction, as it is as illegal to keep wild boar, except in proscribed enclosures, in France as it is in Britain. However, the villagers of Les Vans got together and a petition containing over two hundred signatures caused the ministry to relent. The mayor of Les Vans explained the strength of feeling with typical Gallic logic: 'To Monsieur Evesque, the boar is like a baby.' Such a statement could only have been followed by a large Gallic shrug. (Incidentally, I have heard, but have not managed to verify, that there is a law still valid in France which prevents a pig being named 'Napoleon'.)

However Chirac was not the first instance of a wild boar being adopted as a pet. As long ago as the 1860s, there was a detailed account of such an incident when the writer, Mr F. H. Savin, had been given a wild boar by HH The Maharajah Duleep Singh. The following is an excerpt of an account of her activities after he had had her for six or seven years:

> She follows me almost daily in my walks like a dog, to the great astonishment of strangers. Of course I only take her out when the crops are too low to be injured; during the spring and summer months I merely take her for a run in the park, where she can do no harm. No dog can be more obedient to the whistle than she is. In the heat of summer she is fond of a swim, and has followed me in my boat to a great distance. I always have her belled, to hear where she is in the woods, and the bell, which is a good sheep's bell, is fastened round her neck with a strap and

Ruth Adams of Atlantic City, New Jersey, feeding her pet pig.

buckle. This was of use last autumn, for upon one occasion I lost her for a night or two by her remaining behind with her young ones amongst the acorns; and when I found her by the bell's sound, I was amused to see the immense quantity of rushes which she had collected in a snug dry spot for a lair for herself and family.

Her leaping powers are extraordinary, over water or timber. On one occasion she cleared some palings three feet ten inches in height.

In Devon, a stately obelisk stands overlooking Plymouth as a permanent memorial to a pet pig. Standing thirty feet high, it was erected in the second half of the 18th century by the Countess of Mount Edgcumbe. It is dedicated to 'Cupid', her most faithful companion who would follow her about wherever she went, even accompanying her to London. When he died, he was buried in a gold casket by the obelisk, which then stood in the grounds of Mount Edgcumbe. In the 1860s, it was moved to its present site, overlooking Plymouth Sound.

Dr John Walcot wrote a satirical verse under the pen name of Peter Pindar about the Countess and her 'unusual' dedication to Cupid. He also wrote of a visit to Mount Edgcumbe in 1789 by King George III, standing pensively in front of the grave: 'The Queen from a distance asked him what he was looking at. The King with ready humour replied: "The family vault, Charly, family vault, family vault." '

Having railed against the keeping of pigs as pets, let us finish this section with a quote from the pig-loving G. K. Chesterton's *The Uses of Diversity*:

We do not know what fascinating variations might happen in the pig if once the pig were a pet... You know a Dachshund in the street; you know a St Bernard in the street. But if you saw a Dog in the street you would run from him screaming. For hundreds, if not thousands, of years no one has looked at the horrible hairy original thing called Dog. Why, then, should we be hopeless about the substantial and satisfying thing called Pig? Types of Pig may be differentiated... There may be little, frisky, fighting pigs like Irish or Scotch terriers; there may be little pathetic pigs like King Charles spaniels... Those interested in hair-dressing might amuse themselves by arranging the bristles like those of a poodle... With elaborate training one might have a sheep-pig instead of a sheep-dog, a lap-pig instead of a lap-dog.

The woolly-coated Mangalitza, which can be found in Austria, Hungary, Poland and other Eastern European countries. Some have recently been imported into the UK.

IN 1995 THE GMB Union protested at the 'fat cat' pay rises awarded to Cedric Brown, Chief Executive of British Gas. In order to attract attention, they took along with them to the picket lines a British Saddle-back sow called Cedric, who made headlines again eighteen months later when she farrowed a litter of eight piglets!

Having bitten off part of Evander Holyfield's ear, the former World Heavyweight Boxing Champion, Mike Tyson, was mailed a dozen pig's ears. Sent unwrapped but with the address written on them and stamped, according to a post spokesman, '... they were the weirdest things I have ever seen'.

PIG CELEBRITIES FOR YOUNGSTERS

Alexander and Aunt Pettitoes from *Pigling Bland* by Beatrix Potter.

Arnold Ziffel the Chester White pig that appeared on television in *Green Acres*, a programme shown in America between 1965 and 1971.

Aunts Dorcas and Porcas from *Little Pig Robinson* by Beatrix Potter.

Babe the hero of the 1995 film of the same name. Babe was a Large White with a black coloured topknot. Rescued from an intensive breeding unit to provide a prize at a fair, he is won by an eccentric farmer who encourages the pig to work sheep. The climax of the story is that Babe wins some prestigious sheep dog trials. Based on the book *The Sheep Pig* by Dick King-Smith.

Bertie starred in *Bertie's Escapade*, a lesser known work by Kenneth Grahame, author of *The Wind in the Willows* (1949).

The Black Pig pirate vessel under the command of Captain Pugwash, a popular animated cartoon on children's television in the 1950s, 1960s and 1970s.

Chester the Worldly Pig a book by Bill Peet.

Dan Pig hero of books by Peggy Worville.

Freddy the Pig was the hero of 26 books published between 1927 and 1958, written by Walter R. Brooks in America.

Gloucester the Pig is one of three adventurers in *Pigs May Fly* by Richard W. Farrall (1994).

Grunter the Pig appears in *The Adventures of Sarah and Theodore Bodgitt* by Pamela Oldfield, published 1974.

Gub-Gub was the baby pig featured in *The Story of Doctor Dolittle* by Hugh Lofting (1920) and who also starred in *Gub-Gub's Book* (1932).

Hamm was the piggy bank character in the early 1990s film, *Toy Story*.

Hen Wen is the pig who appears in Lloyd Alexander's 1960s books, such as *The High King*.

➥

Huxley Pig is a character for very young children created by Rodney Peppe, whose books came to television in the 1980s.

Little Pig Robinson was the hero of the book bearing his title by Beatrix Potter published in 1930, which linked Robinson Crusoe with Edward Lear's pig from *The Owl & the Pussycat*.

McMug and McDull are comic cartoon pig characters in Hong Kong.

Miss Piggy is a character originally created by Jim Henson in 1976 for the very successful television series, *The Muppet Show*, and subsequently featured in four films.

Mr Pugstyles is the piggy character in a poem of the same name by writer, poet and dramatist T. S. Eliot.

Paddy Pork is the hero of several picture books created by John S. Goodall during the 1970s.

Padre Porko is a wise and benevolent pig in stories by Robert Davis written in the late 1930s.

Peppa Pig the star of her own television show since 2004 and model for literally tons of children's merchandise.

Peppermint Pig is the title of a book by writer Nina Bawden (1975).

Percy Pig featured in *The Marvellous Adventures of Percy Pig* and *Percy Pig Ahoy!*, written by Rodney Bennett in the early 1940s.

Someone developing an early desire for a pet pig? At Cranleigh Show in 1989.

➥

Peter Pig a Disney character created in 1934, who starred alongside Donald Duck and Mickey Mouse but did not have their staying power.

Peter Pig is a Saddleback who stars in a book of his own name by 'Althea' (1981).

Pigasaurus the pig-like waste disposal unit in the film *The Flintstones*, released in 1994.

Piggins a porcine butler in books such as *Picnic with Piggins* by Jane Yolen.

Piglet featured extensively in the Winnie the Pooh books by A. A. Milne, written during the 1920s.

Pigling Bland and Pig-Wig hero and heroine respectively of *The Tale of Pigling Bland* by Beatrix Potter (1913).

Pigwig is the name of both book and hero by John Dyke, published in 1978.

Piggly featured in *Piggly Plays Truant* by A. J. MacGregor and W. Perring (1946).

Pig Pen was an early character in Charles Schulz's cartoon strip, *Peanuts*.

Pig Plantagenet was the hero of the book of the same name written by Allen Andrews in 1980.

Pinky and Perky were two famous TV puppets, popular in the 1950s and briefly revived in the 1990s. Specialising in song and dance, they were created by Czech-born Jan and Vlasta Dalibor. The original puppets are insured for £1,000,000.

Podgy the porcine friend of Rupert Bear, a cartoon strip that appeared in the *Daily Express* from the 1940s.

Porky hero of a number of Looney Tunes cartoon films from 1935, when he appeared in *I Haven't Got A Hat*. Two years later *Porky's Hare Hunt* introduced us to Bugs Bunny. In later films Porky acquired a girlfriend, Petunia Pig. In all, Porky has appeared in over 160 Warner Brothers cartoons. '*That's all folks!*' was Porky's catch phrase, memorably stuttered by Mel Blanc.

Anthony Henrypottery Luxulyan Prettypig features in Mary and Rowland Emett's *Anthony and Antimacassar* (1943). ➡

Miss Prunella Pig occasional female puppet acquaintance of Pinky and Perky.

Pumbaa is another Disney creation, being the flatulent warthog who appears in *The Lion King*.

Roland the Minstrel Pig is a hero of works by William Steig.

Sam Pig appears in a number of stories by Alison Uttley, published between 1941 and 1960.

Tamworth Pig stars in a series of books from the 1970s by Gene Kemp.

A pair of Tamworth porkers.

The Three Little Pigs started life in a traditional fable but have since come under the wing of the Disney empire, having featured in a series of books by Leonard Leslie Brooke between 1904 and 1922.

Toby Twirl a piglet created by Sheila Hodgetts. He appeared in a large number of books between 1947 and 1956.

Tottie Pig is the hero of a series of books by Vivian French from the 1980s and 1990s.

Wilbur was the star of the book *Charlotte's Web* by E. B. White (1952), which was made into an animated film in 1973, followed by a new, live-action version in 2006.

In case it seems that pigs in these roles are an exclusively Western affair, let me reassure you that *Khryusha*, a Soviet pig puppet, starred for more than twenty years on Communist television in *Good Night Little Ones* until more Americanised children's programmes began to be shown in the 1990s.

Record Breakers

Most Prolific

I have an undated cutting from an anonymous newspaper which, by its appearance and style, might well be from the 1930s. The report is of a sow, Betty, belonging to a Mr Harry S. Pedlingham from Malvern, Worcestershire, who had farrowed 385 pigs in 23 litters. Her 24th litter, at the age of 12, was of two pigs only and Mr Pedlingham was reported to be hoping that she could breed again so that she might achieve a magical 400 offspring in her lifetime. Does anyone know of a more productive pig?

The Swiss are proud of a sow who farrowed three times in one year (1987) producing 54 piglets in a 12-month period. It was reported that her owner thereafter called her 'The Duchess of Pork'.

A litter of Gloucestershire Old Spots suckling.

Largest Single Litter

On 21 September 1993, a cross-bred litter comprising Large White, Duroc and Meishan genes was born totalling 37 piglets at Mr and Mrs M. P. Ford's farm in Yorkshire. Of the litter, 33 survived.

To most pig keepers today, a litter of 20 would still be most unusual and cause for comment. Yet in 1660, Gervaise Markham in his *Cheape and Good Husbandry* laid claim to knowing of one such litter so perhaps pig breeding has not progressed as much as we might like to think, at least in terms of productivity.

To back this up, in 1814, Robert Henderson, in his book *A Treatise On The Breeding Of Swine*, records a litter of 26 'all alive and healthy' being born to a black Chinese sow, belonging to Lady Robert Manners of Sutton, Surrey.

The Smallest Breed

Developed in Italy, mainly for laboratory work, the Mini Maialino has an average adult weight of just 9kgs, or 20lbs.

Largest Pig

The heaviest recorded pig was Big Bill, who weighed 2,552lbs (1158kgs) just before his death in 1933. An American pig, Bill attended agricultural fairs around the country earning his owner, W. J. Chappall, a reasonable income, until he broke a leg en route to the Chicago World's Fair.

Poor Bill was stuffed and mounted and put on display at Weekly County, Tennessee, and then joined a travelling carnival, after which he was supposed to have been donated to a museum. Unfortunately his whereabouts are not now known.

Nebraska Live Stock Remedies of Fremont, Nebraska, made me what I am

NEBRASKA BOY--One of the King Hogs of the World
Weight 1315 Pounds, Age 3 Years

An American postcard depicting another very large pig.

Most Expensive

The highest price paid for a pig in Britain was a modest 4,000 guineas (£4,200) for Foston Sambo 21 when he was sold at auction from the dispersal sale of Mr Andrew Robinson's herd of Gloucestershire Old Spots in Derbyshire in 1994.

This sum somewhat pales into insignificance when compared to the world record of $56,000 for a crossbred called Bud, sold on 5 March 1983 in Hermleigh, Texas, USA.

The Wealthiest

Although not listed by *The Guinness Book of Records* as far as I know, an American pet pig was left the equivalent of £350,000 by his late owner, Margo Lamp, 81, of Davenport, Iowa, to ensure his future comfort, according to a report in the *Sunday Express* in 1990. Does anyone know of a richer pig?

Most Pigs in a Car

Again not recognised in *The Guinness Book of Records*, and not a record I would want anyone to try to beat, but a bizarre story of pig rustling appeared in the British press in 1993. In North Yorkshire, 17 pigs were stolen from a farm and whisked away in the back of a Fiat 127. One can only assume that to get them into such a small vehicle, they must have been only a matter of a couple of weeks old but the court was told that they were worth £884 – or £52 each – which would make them almost pork-weight size or approaching 100kgs each. Methinks someone was telling porkies!

Fastest Pig

In Hamburg, 'Kloten-Joe II' set the land speed record for pigs over 100 metres with a time of 11 seconds.

Biggest Pig Swallowed by a Snake

A 7.32m (24-foot) python swallowed a pig weighing 54.5kg (120lbs) in 1944.

Pig Populations

China is home to 40 per cent of the world's pig population, estimated to be 840,000,000. Of those, 650,000,000 are slaughtered every year for meat.

Largest Piggery

The largest single enterprise keeping pigs is at Timisoara in Romania, which has 70,000 sows producing around 1,200,000 piglets per annum.

THE AGE OF A PIG

We will see elsewhere that the pig is acknowledged to be artful and even sagacious but little has been written about the natural life-span of a pig. This next extract comes from *The Natural History of Selborne* written by Gilbert White in the 1700s. From its description the pig sounds remarkably like a Vietnamese Pot Belly which should not be surprising since oriental pigs were imported around this time to help improve the native types:

'The natural term of a hog's life is little known, and the reason is plain – because it is neither profitable nor convenient to keep that turbulent animal to the full extent of its times: however, my neighbour, a man of substance, who had no occasion to study every little advantage to a nicety, kept a half-bred bantam-sow, who was thick as she was long, and whose belly swept on the ground, till she was advanced to her seventeenth year, at which period she showed some tokens of age by the decay of her teeth and the decline of her fertility.

'For about ten years this prolific mother produced two litters in the year of about ten at a time, and once above twenty at a litter; but, as there were near double the number of pigs to that of teats many died. From long experience in the world this female was grown very sagacious and artful. When she found occasion to converse with a boar she used to open all the intervening gates, where one was kept; and when her purpose was served would return by the same means.'

TOBY THE SAPIENT PIG

By far and away the most famous porcine performer on the boards was Toby, although he was not the first. There was a succession of performing pigs spanning the eighteenth and early nineteenth centuries and doubtless some were more entertaining than others. The performer became known as a 'learned pig' and would do tricks such as spelling, counting, telling the time and reading the thoughts of selected members of the audience.

An early example of such a performing pig was trained by a Mr S. Bisset, a Scottish cobbler who had already trained other performing animals including dogs, monkeys and horses. Starting as a small black weaner, this fellow took 16 months to train and made his debut in 1783.

Such party pieces were described to Dr Samuel Johnson which brought forth the comment in 1784: '… pigs are a race unjustly calumniated! Pig has, it seems, not been wanting to man, but man to pig.'

The following year, the Reverend James Woodforde wrote in his *Diary of a Country Parson*: 'After Dinner the Captain and myself went and saw the learned Pigg… It was wonderful to see the sagacity of the Animal! It was a Boar Pigg, very thin, quite black and with a magic Collar on his Neck. He would spell any word or Numbers from the Letters and Figures that were placed before him.'

The French went one better, as an advertisement from 1793 indicated that a 'surprising learned pig' could articulate the words *'Oui, oui'* with an excellent accent. Cynics might point to the resemblance between these words and a pig's natural tongue and describe the Parisian language as adopting that of the swine, even down to the accent.

Toby first appeared at the St Bartholomew Fair in 1817, an event immortalised in Wordsworth's description of the fair in his poem *The Prelude (Book Seven)*. Billed as 'Toby the Sapient Pig', if the publicity is to be believed he was probably the best of the piggy performers. The following appeared in the *Gloucester Journal* on 28 September, 1818: 'Out in the provinces, Toby could not command the sort of admission fees he brought in London, where it originally cost five shillings to see him, later reducing to half a crown.'

➤

'A peculiarity of the Amazing Pig of Knowledge is that he knew the value of money. He could also tell black from white, distinguish colours, with a shrewd eye count his audience, and even tell people their thoughts.'
– Henry Morley, *Memoirs Of Bartholomew Fair* (1859)

TOBY

THE
SAPIENT PIG,

THE
Greatest Curiosity of the present Day.

THIS MOST EXTRAORDINARY CREATURE
Will Spell and Read, Cast Accounts,
PLAY AT CARDS;
Tell any Person what o'Clock it is to a Minute
BY THEIR OWN WATCH:
ALSO
TELL THE AGE OF ANY ONE IN COMPANY;
And what is more Astonishing he will
Discover a Person's Thoughts,
A Thing never heard of before
To be exhibited by an Animal of the SWINE RACE.
The Performances of this truly SURPRISING CREATURE
must be seen to be believed.
He is now Exhibiting EVERY DAY, at the
Royal Promenade Rooms, Spring Gardens,
Where he may be seen precisely at the Hours of 1, 2, 3, & 4.
ADMITTANCE ONE SHILLING.
Lyon, Printer,   John Street, Edgeware-road.

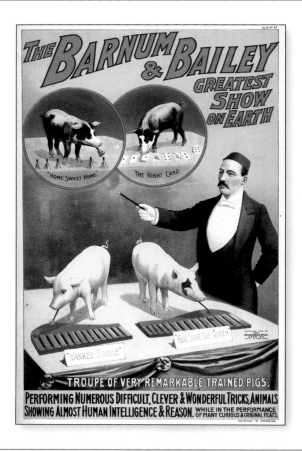

INSPIRATION
FOR MUSICAL INSTRUMENTS

According to the famous film producer/director, Alfred Hitchcock, the squeal of a pig protesting at being carried (as only small pigs can), inspired the creation of one of Britain's most controversial musical inventions:

'I understand the inventor of the bagpipes was inspired when he saw a man carrying an indignant, asthmatic pig under his arm. Unfortunately, the manmade sound never equalled the purity of the sound achieved by the pig.'

Pigs That Rock

All Pigs Must Die – Album by band Death in June.

Apes, Pigs and Spacemen – the name of a band (founded 1995).

A Pork Chop is the Sweetest Flower that Grows – song by Raymond Brown (1903).

Babe: Pig In The City – soundtrack to the film of the same name.

Beatles, The – The groundbreaking musicians of the 1960s used pigs in their songs on more than one occasion. In John Lennon's words in *I Am The Walrus* from the Magical Mystery Tour, there are two references. On the *White Album* was a track entitled *Piggies*, but unusually for The Beatles, written by George Harrison rather than Lennon and McCartney.

Big Pig – Australian band, whose albums include *Bonk*.

Billy Bacon and The Forbidden Pigs – an American band.

Blind Pigs – Brazilian punk rock band formed in 1993.

Blodwyn Pig – Early 1970s British rock band, who released two albums (*Ahead Rings Out* 1970 and *Getting to This* 1971) before splitting in 1972.

Boss Hog – American band who produced an album of the same name.

Cincinnati Dancing Pig – Song recorded by many artists, including Tennessee Ernie Ford.

Fallin' Pork – song by Luigi Pesarest (1906).

Four Wet Pigs – Track on album *The Iowa Waltz* by Greg Brown.

Groundhogs – a British band, whose albums include *Hoggin' The Stage*, *Hogs On The Road* and *Hogwash*.

Ham and Eggs – song by Mike Fitzpatrick in 1922.

Hoggin' A Dub – Album by Manna (Belgian band).

Hog Heaven – Album by Elvin Bishop.

Hog Maw – Track on *The Blue Note Years: 60 Years*, album by various artists.

Hogshead Cheese – Album by blues singers Andy J. Forrest and Kenny Holladay.

Hogs On The Highway – Album by Bad Livers.

Hog Wild – Album by Andy J. Forrest.

Hog Wild – Another, by Hank Williams Jr.

Hurricane – Track by Bob Dylan which included a reference to
a pig circus.

I Can't Lose my Home and my Pork Chops too – song by American
singer Ernest Hogan (1899).

Incredible Hog – British band.

Magnolia Ham Polka – by Charles Ward in 1871.

P.I.G. – Album by Forkeye.

Pig – Raymond Watts's band, with great named albums such as
Praise The Lard.

Pig vs KMFDM – Collaborative effort – albums include *Sin,
Sex and Salvation*.

Pig – Album by Slow Jam.

Pig – Track on album *Volume Two* by Soft Machine.

Pig – Track on *Airport Love Song* by Miss Lum.

Pig – Track on *Si O Si, Que?* by White Trash.

Pig – Found on the album *Coal Chamber* by Coal Chamber.

Pig – Album track on *Sex and Religion* by Steve Vai.

Pig – Album track on *Before These Crowded Streets* by Dave Matthews Band.

Pig And Pepper – A rendering by Sir John Gielgud on a recording of *Alice in Wonderland*.

Pig Ankle Rag – Country track, covered by various bands including Stephen Wade and The Highwoods Stringband.

Pig Ankle Strut – Originally recorded in the 1920s by Gus Cannon.

Pig Bad – Track by Bad Manners from *Fat Sound*.

Pigbag – A fairly obscure British post-punk band.

Pig Blood – Track from *Antibody* by Fetish 69.

Pig Boy – Track on the album *Shihad* by Shihad. The same band had a track on another album called Pig Bop.

Pig Boy – Track on album *Bug Harvest* by Sweaty Nipples.

Pig Brag Crack – Track on the album *Hyderomastgroningem* by Ruins, a Japanese experimental rock duo.

Pig Dance/Ruu Chant – From *Spirit of Polynesia*, an album by various artists.

❖

Pig Dog Daddy – Album track from *From The Ladle To The Grave* by Boiled In Lead.

❖

Pigface – An industrial rock superband, formed in 1990.

❖

Pig Foot And Beer – Track from *Twelve Point Buck/Little Baby Buntin'* by Killdozer.

❖

Pig Foot Pete – From the album *Barrelhouse Boogie & The Blues* by Ella Mae Morse.

❖

Pig Foot Pete – Also to be found on *Blonde Bombshell* by Betty Hutton.

❖

Pig Foot Shuffle – Recorded in the 1920s by Lem Fowler.

Pig Foot Sonata – From the album *1940–41* by Lionel Hampton.

Pig Fucker – Track on the album *REO Speedealer* by the band of the same name.

Pig Fur Elise – From the original soundtrack of the film of *The Butcher Boy* (1997).

Piggy – Musical comedy by C. Friend from 1927.

Piggyback Songs – Compilation album by Kimbo Educational.

Piggy Bank – Song by Les Vandyke (1963).

Piggy Wiggy Woo – Song by A Bear in 1939.

Pig Hollow – Track from the album *The Telling Takes Me Home* by Utah Phillips.

Pig Hunt – From *Land of the Lost* by The Freeze.

Pig In A Blanket – Track on *Death Church* by Rudimentary Peni.

Pig In A Blanket – Also a track on *Our Will Be Done* by The Crucifucks.

Pig In A Can – Track on *Truck Fist* by Daisycutter.

SOW STATUESQUE!

One of the most famous statues must be the brass boar in Florence. The following extract comes from one of the *Fairy Tales* of Hans Christian Andersen, called *The Metal Pig* (1872):

> In the city of Florence, not far from the Piazza del Granduca, runs a little street called Porta Rosa. In this street, just in front of the market place where vegetables are sold, stands a pig, made of brass and curiously formed. The bright colour has been changed by age to dark green; but clear, fresh water pours from the snout, which shines as if it had been polished, and so indeed it has, for hundreds of poor people and children seize it in their hands as they place their mouths close to the mouth of the animal, to drink.

The statue is, in fact, bronze and dates back to 1612 when it was created by P. Tacca. A full-size wild boar sitting on its haunches, it is a copy of the Roman marble statue in the Uffizi Gallery which in turn is a copy of the original Hellenistic sculpture. Situated adjacent to a covered market place at the Loggia del Mercato Nuovo, the locals refer to it as *porcellino* – little pig.

Pig In A Pen – Track on *Church Mountain Country* by Ralph Stanley. A bluegrass favourite, also recorded by a number of other artists.

Pig In A Pin – A track from *Live In Japan* by Spectrum.

Pig In Shit – Track from the album *Ultimatum* by Nightstick.

Pig In The Pen – Track from *Tennessee Jubilee* by Benny Martin.

Pig Iron – Track on *Scum* by Anti-Nowhere League.

Pig Iron Peggy – Track on *Ghost Of The Willow Grove* by JD Beard.

Pig Iron Sally – Recorded in the 1930s by Lucille Bogan.

Pig Kingdom Come – From the album *Sum Of The Men* by Man Is The Bastard.

Pig Knuckled Down – Track on the album *Machinery Hill* by Flour.

Pig Latin – From *Making Things With Light* by Mr T Experience.

Pig Latin – On the album *Seasick* by Imperial Teen.

Pig Latin Love Song – From *Mama U-Seapa* by Steve Ferguson & the Midwest Creole.

Pig Latin Song – Track on *Leadbelly's Last Sessions* by Leadbelly.

Piglets – A one-hit wonder, British all-girl group from the Jonathan King stable, whose record *Johnny Reggae* reached number three in the charts in 1971 and became a sort of cult anthem for British Hells Angels thereafter.

Pigmeat – From *Leadbelly Memorial Volumes 1 & 2* by Leadbelly.

Pigmeat Blues – Widely recorded blues standard appearing on albums by Georgia Tom, Tiny Parham & The Blues Singers, Clifford Hayes etc.

Pigmeat Is What I Crave – Recorded by Bo Carter in the 1930s.

Pig Meat Mama – Recorded by Mae Glover in the 1930s.

Pigmeat Markham – A black American comedian who appeared on the 1960s television programme *Rowan & Martin's Laugh-in* and who recorded several albums including *Here Comes The Judge*, his catch-phrase.

Pigmeat On The Line – Recorded by Memphis Minnie in the 1940s.

Pigmeat Papa – Another blues recording, by Georgia Tom from the 1920s.

Pig Meat Strut – A blues standard probably most closely associated with Big Bill Broonzy from the 1920s.

Pig No Swig – Track on the album *Glass Cockpit* by House of Large Sizes.

Pig 'n Whistle Red – Album by Blind Willie McTell, a hugely influential US blues singer of the 20th C.

Pig Off Ass Full – From the album *Vedder Vedder Bed Wetter* by To Live & Shave In LA.

Pig On The Engine – From *Natasha's Waltz* by Norman and Nancy Blake.

Pig Organ, The – A comic opera performed at London's The Round House in 1980, telling the story of swineherd Otto and his musical piglets. Bizarre instruments included a Sausage Drum, a Belliphon, Swionin, Pig Pipes and a Xylotrotter.

Pig Or Pup (or The Two-faced Man) – Recorded by Rev Emmett Dickenson, c. 1930.

Pig Out – Album by Frank Allison and Odd Sox.

Pigpen – 1990s band, whose albums include *Miss Ann*.

Pigpen – Nickname of Ronald C. McKernan, a founding member of 1970s band, Grateful Dead.

Pig Pen – Track on EP *Licker Bottle Cozy* by Grinspoon.

Pig Pen Boogie – Track on the album *S/T* by Pax.

Pig Pile – Album by Big Black.

Pig Politics – Track from *Hei-Wa Hoedown* by Walt Koken.

Pig Power – From the original soundtrack of the 1995 film *Gordy*, the tale of a talking pig.

Pig Power – From *Kool Songs* by Kangaroo Kids.

Pig Pretty – Album by Heave.

Pigs – Track from *Animals* by Pink Floyd.

Pigs – German band.

Pigs Apes – UK band.

Pigs Can See The Wind – Folksong by Dave Goulder on the album *Harbors of Home*.

Pigs Are People Too – Album by Fitz of Depression.

Pig Secrets – Album track from *Velocity* by Penniless People of Bulgaria.

Pigs Is Pigs – Song by Gertrude Campbell (written 1907).

Pig's In Zen – From *Nothing's Shocking* by Jane's Addiction.

Pigsix 5 – German band.

Pig's Last Stand – Album by Poison Idea.

Pig Snoots and Nehi Red – Album track from *Watchin' TV* by Barefoot Jerry.

Pigs On The Wing – Another track on *Animals* by Pink Floyd.

Pigs & Battleships – Album by Quando Quango.

Pig Storm – From *Nuclear Nightclub* by Wigwam.

Pig Sweat – Track from *Right Now* by Pussy Galore.

Pig Tails – Track from *Barbados Sweet Fuh Days*, a compilation album by various artists.

Pig Tail Swing – Track on *School Bus* by Bob Log III.

Pig Town Fling – Track from *First Harvest: Ten Years Of Acorn Music* by Tony & Peter Elman.

Pig Trotters – From the album *The Darlings of Wapping Wharf Launderette* by Small Faces.

Pig Until Proven Cop – Track on *Available In All Colors* by One Minute Silence.

Pig Valentine – Album by Sixty Foot Dolls.

Pig Virus – From *Private Parts* by Howard Stern.

Pigwalk – Album by Stuck Mojo.

Pork and Beans – Ragtime two-step by Bennet Thomas (1909).

Serious Solid Swineherd – German band.

Steam Pig – A 1980s German band.

Swine – Track on the album *Embrace The Eternal* by Embodyment.

Swine – Track on the album *Crunt* by Crunt.

Swine – Another from *The Juliet Letters* by Elvis Costello.

Swinebarn No.3 – Track on *IGL Rock Story Part 2 (1967–68)*,
a compilation album.

Swine Dive – Track on the album *High Wire Act* by Pry.

Swine Eyed Sheep – Track on *Token Remedies Research* by Damaged.

Swine Shrieks – Track on *Sounds of Bamboo* by Solomon Islands.

Swine Song – Track on *Toxic Voodoo* by Fear of God.

The Boar Hunt – By William Smith (1890).

The Boar Is Dead – Song by Arthur Harris in 1955.

The Ham Tree Barbecue – By Jean Schwartz (1905).

The Peasant's Triumph on the Death of the Wild Boar – Three dances by Thomas Arne, 1741.

The Pig Theme – Track on the album *The Underground Railroad To My Heart* by Fred Houn and the Afro-Asian Music Ensemble.

The Sow Took The Measles – song featured in the Folksinger's Wordbook.

The Tasty Bits of Crackling on the Pork – By Felix Macglennon (1898).

The Three Little Pigs Are Pork Chops Now – Song by Jas Hanley, 1934.

Did anyone hear huffing and puffing?

War Pigs – Track on Black Sabbath's album, *Paranoid*.

❖

Wart Hog – Track on the album *Too Tough To Die* by The Ramones.

❖

When Pigs Fly – Band who produced an album of the same name.

❖

Wild Boar – One of the songs recorded by Flanders & Swann.

❖

Wild Boar – From the album *Where The Sidewalk Ends* by Shel Silverstein.

Wild Boar Problem – Track on the album *Carrots & So On* by Nevada Bachelors.

❖

You Can't Get Many Pimples on a Pound of Pickled Pork – Song by Fred Fischer (1905).

❖

To close this musical section, ponder a moment on the following news item from *Farmers Weekly* in October 2001:

> Farmers are playing Britney Spears CDs to scare off troublesome wild boars in Germany, reports the *Daily Record*. Farmer Hermann-Josef Becker tried music because he was unable to shoot the animals as they are a protected species. He said: 'Madonna didn't work too well. Robbie Williams was a dead loss but they can't stand Britney Spears.'

THE INSCRIPTION ON
A GRAVESTONE IN
ST MARY'S CHURCH, CHELTENHAM

Here lies John Higgs
A famous man for killing pigs,
For killing pigs was his delight,
Both morning, afternoon and night.
Both heats and colds he did endure,
Which no physician could ere cure.
His knife is laid, his work is done;
I hope to heaven his soul has gone.

A Welsh gilt.

HOG THE HERO 3

The Tamworth Two

What makes someone or something heroic or even newsworthy can often be a puzzle. In January 1998, two rather anonymous cross-bred pigs escaped from an abattoir in rural Wiltshire and not only grabbed the nation's headlines and attention for no fewer than four days but also gained significant press coverage abroad. Now their escapade has been made into a film!

What is curious is that there are other escapees from abattoirs who never gain more than a brief paragraph at the bottom of an inside page of the local weekly newspaper. Some do not even warrant that. I have known of bullocks that have remained free for longer and travelled further than either Butch Cassidy or Sundance (as the two pigs were dubbed by the popular press) but whose exploits were never even fleetingly acknowledged in the media.

The pigs' story did not make the national press until the 14 January, by which time they had evaded capture for six days. The two ginger-coloured runaways had made their escape from Newman's abattoir in Malmesbury, Wiltshire, by swimming across the River Avon and then making their way to freedom through back gardens and allotments, both of which afforded plenty of possibilities for young pork-weight pigs to keep up their daily calorie intake.

The news itself spawned the sort of activity that these rural parts of north Wiltshire experience only once or so in a century. Local hotels and hostelries were soon fully booked by journalists, photographers and camera crews and locals were elbowed aside at the bars of the village pubs in the evenings. The police and RSPCA, of course, were involved and local characters of various shades of colourfulness, doubtless often recruited in those self-same village pub bars, came forward to lend their expertise. One brought along his 'sixty stone' Tamworth sow on a harness and lead and paraded her up and down beside a copse where the fugitives had recently been spotted, in the certain belief that they would be unable to resist the charms of this big red-headed lady – but this theory was shown to be flawed.

➳

A Tamworth sow.

After four days of so-called experts and officials and the media chasing around in hired pick-ups, the two pigs decided enough was enough and allowed themselves to be recaptured. It was reported on the 17 January that Sundance had been taken after a third tranquilliser dart had penetrated his hide and slowed him sufficiently to be caught by a vet with a noose and the story was almost over, with Butch having succumbed the previous day. One piece of irony not lost on the press was that Sundance's tranquillised body was taken off to a vet's surgery to recover in a van marked 'Quality Meats'.

The two pigs, estimated to be worth around £40 each as part of the food chain, now became a serious investment for their road-sweeper owner, Arnoldo Dijulio. The *Daily Mail* eventually won the bidding war with a sum said to be in the thousands and in typical style promised their readers that the pigs would be looked after regally for the rest of their natural lives. Thus they were moved to an animal sanctuary and a farm park before finding long-term peace at the South of England Rare Breeds Centre at Woodchurch, near Ashford in Kent. That these two pigs should become so valuable and have their lives spared, while literally thousands of others are slaughtered for food to make the pork chops and bacon sandwiches consumed as readily by *Mail* employees and readers as anyone, is just one more conundrum in this strange little tale that made heroes out of two rather ordinary Tamworth-cross pigs. ➤

Something that was overlooked by journalists at the time was a report that had appeared about a year before the escape took place. The local paper, the *Wilts and Gloucestershire Standard*, had reprinted, as part of a regular series, a piece of news from 75 years earlier – 1922. This was a court report about a Crudwell farmer who had been charged and fined for allowing his pig to stray on to the public highway. He pleaded that someone had left the gate open and that he could not be expected to check it all the time, but the magistrates ruled that 'it was exceedingly dangerous in these days of motor traffic to allow pigs to get on the road' and fined him 2s 6d (12p). I wonder if any of the many 1998 pig-pursuing policemen, enjoying the change in routine, ever thought to prosecute the escapees' owner, or the abattoir?

SOW INSULTING!

George Bernard Shaw's work attracted its fair share of brittle critical acclaim. The following is an extract from a review of the play *Mrs Warren's Profession* from 1905:

> Superabundance of foulness… wholly immoral and
> degenerate… you cannot have a clean pig sty.

Oh, but you can.

American writer Ralph Waldo Emerson seems to have had a low opinion of the British aristocracy according to *English Traits*, written in 1856:

> Twenty thousand thieves landed at Hastings. These founders
> of the House of Lords were greedy and ferocious dragoons, sons
> of greedy and ferocious pirates. Such, however, is the illusion of
> antiquity and wealth, that decent and dignified men now exist-
> ing, boast their descent from these filthy thieves, who showed a
> far juster conviction of their own merits, by assuming for their
> types the swine, goat, jackal, leopard, wolf, and snake, when they
> severally assembled.

GARDENING WITH PIGS

The gardeners had told the Prince that you couldn't have pigs and flowers, so he decided to have pigs.
– Saki, *The Storyteller* (1914)

The ancient Egyptians used pigs to tread in the corn. In well-cultivated fields, where the soil was soft and pliable, the seed corn was scattered and pigs subsequently turned out and driven around the field by boys with sticks. Thus, the sharp pointed feet of the pigs created indentations for the cereal to settle in and germinate. As the pigs were driven, they never had the chance to stop and feed on the corn or turn up the ground with their snouts.

In modern times, a newspaper report tells of a relation of the journalist concerned who, each autumn, reverts to the ancient custom of cotters by fencing off his vegetable patch, buying in a couple of weaners and leaving them to do all the digging and fertilising necessary. After three months, the soil is well rested from cultivation, manured and turned over, allowing the frost to finish the work. The pigs, meanwhile, are fattened and ready for the butcher. It sounds a lot easier and more rewarding than digging. And pigs, who turn over the soil in search of roots, are much more efficient at clearing the ground of tenacious weeds such as couch grass and ground elder.

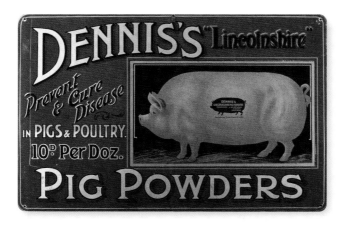

MILKING YOUR PIG

Let us now consider another possible agricultural application for the pig. Nearly every farm animal is milked by someone somewhere. Most common of course are the cow and the goat but the sheep comes in a close third, with specialist breeds being developed for milking for cheese production. Roquefort, for example, is a famous French soft, blue cheese made from ewe's milk.

Other animals used are the bison (for true Parmesan cheese), the camel and the horse (in Mongolia). But where is our porcine hero?

In the late eighteenth/early nineteenth century, it was reported by the local British Embassy that travellers to the province of Canton in China were being given pig's milk to drink. There was, of course, no problem until the source was discovered, as pig's milk is perfectly nutritious. However a general abhorrence of the idea created an outcry from visiting Westerners. An engraving from the Victorian era shows that the idea, at least, was taken further and practical methods of milking pigs were being considered.

The ancient Greeks and Romans were, apparently, familiar with the consumption of pig's milk, though Plutarch tells us that those who drank it became blotchy and leprous.

Notwithstanding the possibility of skin complaints, the sow has an undeniably generous udder and is capable of providing between seven and 14 pints a day. Analysis of pig's milk shows that it carries more fat than either cow's or human's (though less than either ewe's or goat's), but has a lower level of milk sugar than any of them. The fat globules are about a quarter the size of those from a cow and there are about eight times as many of them, which means that on both counts, pig's milk is ideally suited to making cheese.

Problems arise, as the Victorians undoubtedly discovered, in finding the means to extract the milk profitably. All the other creatures listed as providing milk for human consumption have a regulation four teats, which makes the provision of machinery to deal with the task relatively easy. The pig is different. Unlike all the others, the sow regularly has multi-births of as many as 20-odd piglets (instances of as many as 37 have been recorded), and to meet these needs nature has given her a much larger milk

➳

bar than the others. However, the number of teats or dills has never been constant and some sows may have 12, others 14, or even 16 or 18. This obviously complicates the machinery design. Also, pigs have more control over their milk's release than other creatures and only 'let down' their milk at a given stimulus which would be difficult to replicate in a machine.

However, when man can put his fellows on the moon and bring them back again or produce the abilities of a multifunctional computer on a microchip, is this really an excuse? Truth to tell, the technology could be found if there was a market begging for the product but today's customer is as likely to be as squeamish as those past travellers to Canton. Here in the West, there is no real shortage either of milk sources to meet the demand for butter, yoghurt, cheese and fresh milk, so sow's milk is likely to remain as solely a source of nourishment for countless piglets yet to come!

American scientists have different ideas, though. With the advent of genetic engineering, experts in Boston have created a pig whose milk contains an anti-clotting protein, which, it is hoped, will be extracted and used to help prevent blood clotting in the fight against human heart disease.

Incidentally, it was a long-held belief among German country folk that adding pig's milk to a wife-beater's diet would cure him of his brutality.

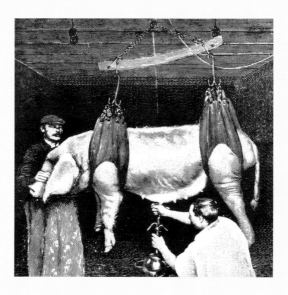

THE PIG BOOK – AN EDWARDIAN PARLOUR GAME

There was a fad, roughly from the 1890s to the end of World War I, at dinner parties especially, to blindfold guests and get them to draw a pig. Indeed, special books could be bought for just this purpose, with space for the drawing and for the name of the artist and the date. Some of the representations of pigs were better and more recognisable than others, of course.

In many cases, famous people of the time were persuaded to join in. The following is one taken from just such a book entitled *The Philippine Pig Book*, dated 1899, which included attempts by a number of luminaries including this one by Winston Churchill.

It should perhaps not be surprising that the future Prime Minister's efforts were more than recognisably porcine, albeit one fairly dangerous-looking animal. It is well recorded that Winston often signed his frequent letters to his beloved wife, Clementine, with a small drawing of a pig. *The Philippine Pig Book* went under the hammer in 1981 and sold for a substantial sum.

Winston Churchill's porker from The Philippine Pig Book.

CEREMONIAL DUTIES

A pig is not often chosen as a regimental mascot. The goat or dog is much more likely to be on duty during pomp and pageantry occasions but in the 1920s the Royal Inniskillings did have a famous porcine mascot, Muriel. Muriel was house-trained and a keen jogger, joining in all sorts of army activities including demonstration bayonet charges. The regiment was posted to Iraq and rather than take her to such inhospitable climes, she was given to some gunners to look after. Instead, they ate her for their Christmas lunch.

More Piggy Mascots:

*It is positively affecting to see how the sailors of
HMS Glasgow in 1909 took fancy to their ship's mascot,
a large sow named Trotter.*
– Rev J.G. Wood, *Petland Revisited*

*Would any regiment like as a gift from a lady a little
tame white pig for a mascot? Two months old; hand
fed; very affectionate.*
– From *The Times*, 8 January 1916

In America, the Saint Paul (Minnesota) Saints minor league baseball team have had a pig as a mascot since 1993. The pig, replaced annually, carries new baseballs in a specially made harness and accompanies the team to all games.

HOG THE HERO 4

Priscilla the Pig Day

In 1984, a pet pig, Priscilla, belonging to Victoria Herberta, saved a drowning boy at Lake Somerville, Texas, by jumping into the water, swimming to the child and allowing him to hold on to her harness while both swam back to shore. Twice, both pig and boy went under but the shore was safely reached and the boy saved. The American Humane Association recognised this act of heroism and awarded Priscilla its Stillman Award. Going one better, the Mayor of Houston announced an official '*Priscilla the Pig Day*' and she became the first member of the Texas Pet Hall of Fame.

Priscilla's owner was a pig fanatic, and her house and garden were bedecked with models and symbols of pigs. Her address became 'Hog Heaven, Pigdom, Texas' while Priscilla went on the celebrity circuit, appearing on television in nail varnish and eye shadow. The hog hero even opened the International Belly Flop Contest at the University of Illinois.

Yet all this attention was to turn sour for Victoria Herberta. She also owned a boar son of Priscilla's, Jerome by name, but as he grew to maturity the same Houston authorities ruled that he was unclean and could no longer be kept as a pet. This was in spite of a claim by his owner that he was bathed every day and that she even cleaned his teeth twice daily. But officialdom ruled and Jerome was sent away to the farm where Priscilla was bred, only to start pining as soon as his doting mistress departed. He lost so much weight that she gave up her home and moved to the farm to be with him, for two years. After that time, she decided that she really must return home again and left the farm, immediately triggering another bout of self-starvation in the pig. One night, soon after her departure, there was a storm and Jerome, uncharacteristically for his species, went outside where he was struck by lightning. Victoria Herberta vowed that she would never have another pig.

A Hog By Any Other Name

Aardvark – Earth pig [*Aard* = earth, *vark* = pig (Dutch African)]

Giant hogweed – *Heracleum mantegazzianum,* an umbellifer which favours river banks and grows to a huge size

Hog – A brush for cleaning the underparts of a boat or larger vessel

Hog – A machine for chipping timber into firewood

Hog ape – The baboon

Hogback – In golf, a ridge surrounding a hole or on a fairway

Hog-nosed skunk – A type of skunk with a flattened nose

Hog-nose snake – A snake with a snout-like nose

Hogs Fennel – According to Gervaise Markham in 1660, a weed that grows among corn; also known as Mayth. (More recently, it is an alternative name for Sea Sulphurwort, a weed growing on salt marshes)

Hogshead – A barrel containing approximately 52½ gallons

Hogsucker – A freshwater fish found in the eastern US. Also known as hogmolly.

Hog tie – To incapacitate by tying the legs together

Hogweed – Also known as Cow Parsnip. It was once valued as a food for pigs so that children were sent out into the hedgerows to harvest it for the pig at home.

Hog wild – To be out of control

Intelligent pigs – Electronic robots used to travel down pipelines to detect faults and blockages

Iron hog – The literal translation of the Dutch word for porcupine

Pig – A lump of rock salt

Pig – A mould for producing lead or iron (hence pig-iron)

Pig – An earthenware vessel

Pig – A one-ton Humber armoured personnel carrier, first made in the 1940s and still in use by the British army in the late 1980s

Pig – A parcel of hemp fibre (weighing roughly 1kg)

Pig – A piece of lead used for ship's ballast

Pig – A sixpenny piece

Pig – A small cushion used in knitting

Piggly Wiggly® – The first American self-service store group set up in Memphis, Tennessee in 1916 by Clarence Saunders

Pig-in-the-hedge – Blackthorn

Pig Island – Ireland, known since early times as *Muic-inis*

Pig Latin – A form of code where the initial consonant of each word is transposed to the end of that word with '-ay' added to finish the word. Thus 'long pig' becomes *onglay igpay*. Widely used by children to maintain peer group secrecy, it dates back to the late 1500s.

Piglet of St John – Wood louse in Italian (*porcello di San Giovanni*)

Pig-lily – Arum lily

Pig-man, Pig-wife – Someone who sells crockery (Scotland)

Pignut – Earth nut

Pig-puzzle – A gate which swings both ways

PIGS – Abbreviation for Portugal, Italy, Greece, Spain (also sometimes PIIGS when including Ireland), the weakest Eurozone economies in the 2008–10 recession.

Pig's Bubble (also Pig's Cole, Pig's Flop) – Cow Parsnip

Pig's Ear – Biting Stonecrop

Pig's Eye – Cuckoo Flower

Pig's Foot (also Pig's Pettitoes) – Birdsfoot Trefoil

Pig's Grass (also Pig-Rush, Pig-Weed) – Knotgrass

Pigskin – A saddle

Pig's Mouth (also Pig's Chops) – Toadflax

Pig's Nose – A variety of apple and a rose hip; a brand of Scotch whisky

Pig's Snout – A variety of apple

Pig's Tail – Goosegrass

Pigstick – A short spear used in hunting wild boar

Pig Weed – Fat Hen or Goosefoot

Pirlie Pig (also Purlie Pig or Pinner Pig) – Scottish onion-shaped pottery vessel for saving coins, 15th–19th C

Porcelain – From the Italian *porcella*, a young sow, due to the shape of a pig's back and the smooth pink surface

Quilly-pig – Porcupine

Salt pig – A container for salt made from clay

Sea hog – The porpoise

Sow and Pigs – A long mould with smaller moulds leading off it for casting iron or lead

Sow's Tits – The plant Solomon's Seal

Sow Thistle (also Hogweed, Swine-thistle) – A common weed of the daisy family

Swamp hog – Nickname for the capybara, a large South American rodent that inhabits swampy areas

Swine – The name of a looping rollercoaster planned for the end of Southend Pier in Essex (biggest ever)

Swine-cress – Wart-cress

Swine flu – The influenza A, H1N1 virus, blamed on Mexican pigs that created the 2009 pandemic that never was

Swine's Snout – Dandelion

A Middle White sow.

HOG THE HERO 5

Tirpitz

'Tirpitz' was the name given to this heroic hog from World War I. Tirpitz was awarded an Iron Cross, albeit by sailors on a Royal Naval vessel, survived indescribable red tape in order to enter the British Isles and then raised firstly £200 and then £400 in aid of the British Red Cross before slipping into obscurity. Tirpitz was a 'pet' pig kept on board HMS *Dresden*. During the Falkland Islands battle, the *Dresden* sank, apparently having been scuttled by her crew, on 14 March 1915. They escaped leaving Tirpitz as the only crew member not to abandon ship. HMS *Glasgow* arrived on the scene and brought Tirpitz aboard, the crew awarding him the Iron Cross for his devotion to duty.

The Petty Officer who had first spotted the pig swimming around the stricken *Dresden* claimed ownership of him and the *Glasgow* eventually returned to Portsmouth some eighteen months later. The ship's captain signalled the Commander-in-Chief, requesting permission to land the pig, but the matter was referred to the Admiralty and then on to the Ministry of Agriculture before a decision could be made.

Eventually, temporary accommodation was built on Portsmouth jetty to house the pig whilst he underwent the requisite quarantine. But the jetty at Portsmouth was not the ideal place in wartime and plans were eventually agreed to transfer Tirpitz to a piggery on nearby Whale Island. This too did not pass off without incident. The pig was loaded on to a cutter and secured in place with a net but the cutter broke free from its tow just as a sea fog blew up and Tirpitz was left drifting in the waters off the south coast of England while search parties were scrambled to find him.

Eventually he reached his new home, joining the other pigs at Whale Island. There he stayed until one day the Petty Officer arrived, demanding his spoils of war. Tirpitz was duly handed over and was taken back to the sailor's home in Yorkshire. In due course, the Petty Officer was again called up to rejoin the fleet and he decided to raffle the now famous Tirpitz to raise funds for the Red Cross, which he did, raising over £200.

A newspaper report shows that Tirpitz was (again?) raffled in Wiltshire in aid of the British Red Cross on the instructions of Commodore Luce (late Captain of HMS *Glasgow*) by Messrs Knight Frank and Rutley in December 1917. The sale took place at Malmesbury and raised 400 guineas – so Tirpitz truly helped the British war effort.

THE DISCOVERY OF THE SPA AT BATH

Although not modern, the discovery of the invigorating waters at Bath is credited to a herd of pigs and since this is one of the earliest documented recordings of pig husbandry in Britain, being 863 BC, it is worth recording here in some detail.

Baldred, eldest son of Lud Hudibras (then King of Britain), it is said, having spent eleven years at Athens in study, came home leprous, and was in consequence confined to prevent infection. Having effected his escape, however, he went very remote from his father's court, into an untrammelled part of the country, and offered his services in any common employment. He entered into service at Learwick, a small village three miles from Bath, where his business was to take care of the pigs, which he was to drive from place to place for their advantage in feeding upon acorns, haws, etc. While at his usual employment one morning, a part of the drove of swine, as if seized with a frenzy, ran down the side of a hill into an elder-moor, till they reached the spot of ground where the hot springs of Bath now boil up, and from thence returned, covered with black mud. The prince being of a thoughtful turn, was very desirous to find out the reason why the pigs that wallowed in the mire in summer to cool themselves, should do the same in winter; at length, he perceived a steam arise from the place where they had wallowed, and making his way to it, found it warm. Having thus satisfied himself that it was for the benefit of the heat that the pigs resorted hither, he observed, that after a while they became whole and smooth from their scabs and eruptions by often wallowing in this mud. Upon this, he considered within himself why he should not receive the same benefit by the like means. He tried the experiment with success, and finding himself cured of his leprosy, declared who he was. His master, though incredulous at first, being at last persuaded to believe him, went with him to court, where he was owned; and upon succeeding to his father, he erected the baths.

In one of these baths there is at the present time a statue of King Baldred, which was erected in 1699, under which is the following inscription on copper:

➤

— 150 —

Baldred, son of Lud Hudibras, eighth King of the Britons from Brute, a great philosopher and mathematician, bred at Athens, and recorded the first discoverer and founder of these baths, 863 years before Christ.

Alas, like his son, King Lear, Baldred (or Bladud), did not have a happy ending. Slipping increasingly into senility, he became convinced he could fly and died proving it when he jumped off the pinnacle of a temple he had built to the Celtic goddess, Sulis. On the approach to Bath on the old A46, watch out for the 'Bladud Arms' with its sign of Bladud with his pigs.

SOW STATUESQUE!

Situated in Newport, Gwent, this delightful bronze is located outside the town's covered market. It shows a sow of the Welsh breed carrying a pannier of fruit, presumably to deter the local youth from using the statue as a resting place while awaiting the next omnibus.

The inscription calls it 'This Little Pig Went to Market' and it was commissioned in the 1990s to mark 700 years of market trading in Newport.

PIGS ON SCREEN

In recent films, 'Betty' starred in *A Private Function* (1984) and pigs feature heavily in Leon The Pig Farmer (1993). The film Misery (1991), based on a Stephen King novel, features the frightening Annie Wilkes who keeps a fully grown pig as a pet. *The Hour of the Pig* (1994) was concerned largely with the public trials of pigs in the Middle Ages and used Iron Age pigs from the Cotswold Farm Park to depict the animals of that era. Probably the best-known pig film today though, is *Babe*, a groundbreaking children's film, beloved by many adults too, made in 1995. With the use of computer graphics and extremely well-trained animals, it is entirely possible to believe that the creatures are actually talking. Forty-eight pigs were trained as shooting took so long that to maintain a constant size throughout, different batches of pigs were needed of different ages. Strangely, although Babe is constantly referred to in the film as 'he' and 'him', all the pigs featured are very obviously female! The follow-up film, *Babe in the City*, was not based on a Dick King-Smith book like the first but on a commissioned film script and it was less of a hit.

One of the earliest on-screen pigs was 'Blue Boy', a Hampshire, which starred with Will Rogers in the 1933 film, *State Fair*, a musical by Rodgers and Hammerstein.

Other films featuring pigs include *Das Fröhliche Dorf*, a German film from 1955; *Futz*, released in 1969; *Grisjakten*, a Swedish satire from 1970; *Razorback*, an Australian not-very-frightening horror film from 1984; Disney's *The Black Cauldron* (1985); *Wawa*, a Taiwanese children's film from 1991; and *Garfield and Friends* from 1988, in which Orson the pig joins the popular cat from the long-running comic strip.

BEDBUGS

It has been reported that, if you are travelling to some of the more exotic countries where the heat of the day quickly vanishes and where you might just find some hungry bedbugs under the blankets, you can do a lot worse than pop a pig into the bed several hours before turning in. The result is that the bed is warmed and the bed bugs fully fed – but remember to turf the pig out before you take your rightful place.

A PRIVATE FUNCTION

The film *A Private Function* (1984) was an endearing tale about post-war, food-rationed Britain where a middle class couple, played by Michael Palin and Maggie Smith, tried to kidnap a pig intended for the town's celebration of Princess Elizabeth's impending marriage. A witty script by Alan Bennett demonstrates the problems and disadvantages of trying to hide a pig at home.

To reinforce the message that pigs were never intended as pets, it is worth recounting here Michael Palin's observations when the script called for him to share his car with the pig. In trying to escape, it all but castrated him with its hind trotters at the same time evacuating its bowels into his lap. In summing up the experience, the former *Monty Python* star likened it to trying to get a Sumo wrestler out of an igloo.

My Mum says I can't come out to play today.

PIG MONSTERS

Catoblepas Originally described by Pliny as inhabiting the Nile, the beast was later described as a black buffalo with the head of a pig which would render one dead if one so much as glimpsed its eyes.

Chancha con cadenas Or the 'sow harnessed with chains', is a modern myth from Argentina. The creature makes a frightening din as it makes its way along railway tracks or telegraph wires. Otherwise known as Tin Pig (*chancho de lata*).

Curupira From Brazil, an ugly dwarf with one eye, a bald head, large ears and a hairy body, always seen riding a pig with his feet turned backwards. Surprisingly, despite his appearance, he was benevolent.

Cynocephalia A tribe from the East Indies, according to Robert Burton's *Miracles of Art and Nature*. They were supposed to have hogs' teeth growing from their snouts and from behind their ears.

Eale An Indian monster the size of a hippo with an elephant's tail and the jaws of a wild boar. His special feature was his moveable horns, one of which he could roll up and keep in reserve lest the other was damaged.

Erymanthian Boar From Greek mythology, this huge boar ravaged the countryside of Mount Erymanthus where it dwelt until it was attended to by Heracles, in the fourth of his labours.

Four-Footed Whale A heraldic monster with a boar's head and tusks, a row of spikes down its body and four clawed feet.

Glawackus A modern American mythical creature, variously resembling a lion, a cougar, a panther or a boar. Sightings reported in Glastonbury, Connecticut, in 1939 and Frizzelburg, Maryland, in 1944 where it reputedly fought a bull.

Gorgon The Gorgon was said to come from Africa and a truly frightening beast it must have been. Its porcine connection was in having the teeth of a boar but the rest was made up of dragon's scales, wings, the bloodshot eyes of an ox with heavy eyelids, a long and heavy mane which covered the front of its face, and hands, all in the body of a small bull. It was believed to be real as recently as the 16th century.

➤

Hog Fish or Ambize A fish monster from the Congo with a fish's body, the muzzle of an ox, hands and a tail shaped like a target. It would grow up to 500lbs in weight and when eaten, tasted like pork.

Kamapua'a From Hawaiian mythology, the name means 'hog-child'. Before becoming a deity, the Kamapua'a turned up the earth with his snout making a defensive hill for the gods. He developed into a benign, brave and strong god, protecting the people and doing battle for good. His adventures ranged between the amorous and the warlike.

Merrows A people from Ireland who lived on dry land below the sea. Whilst the women were very beautiful, the men had green hair and teeth, with a red nose and piggy eyes.

Mome Raths From Lewis Carroll's *Through the Looking Glass*, where Humpty Dumpty describes them thus: 'Well, a "rath" is a sort of green pig: but "mome" I'm not certain about. I think it's short for "from home" – meaning they'd lost their way, you know.'

> 'Twas brillig, and the slithy toves
> Did gyre and gimble in the wabe:
> All mimsy were the borogoves,
> And the mome raths outgrabe.

Monoceros Described by Pliny, it had the body of a horse, a stag's head with a single horn about a foot long, like that of a unicorn, elephant's feet and a boar's tail. It was said that it could never be taken alive.

Nependis A heraldic beast, half ape, half pig.

Pantheon Another heraldic creature based on a panther but with feet cloven like a hog's.

Piggiwiggia Pyramidalis A creation of Edward Lear's, being a plant with flowers in the form of pigs.

Ping-Feng From China, a monster with the body of a black pig with a human head at either end.

St Attracta's Monster A beast from Ireland which had boar's tusks, fiery eyes, ram's ears and roared like a lion but which died when St Attracta made the sign of the cross over it.

Sea Hog Reported in the North Sea in 1537, it had the head of a hog with teeth and tusks of a boar, 'a bending back like a creature begotten by swine', four dragon's legs and the tail of a fish. Considered to be very vicious.

Twrch Trywth The fearsome giant boar in the Welsh legends of King Arthur. It had once been a king but had been transformed into a boar by God as a punishment.

Unicorn Whilst we all know the unicorn to be a white, horse-like creature with a single, spiralling horn on the forehead, Julius Solinus gives a fuller description, viz: 'the cruellist is the Unicorne, a monster that belloweth horriblie, bodyed like a horse, footed like an Elephant, tayled like a Swine, and headed like a Stagge. His horne sticketh out of the midds of his forehead, of a wonderful brightness about foore foote long, so sharp that whatsoever he pusheth at, he striketh it through easily.'

Varaha The Hindu belief of Vishnu's incarnation as a boar; as such he saved the world from Hiranyaksha, who had stolen the earth and taken it to the bottom of the ocean. Consequently, the earth rests on his tusks and earthquakes are the result of his shifting position.

Verethraghna The boar belonging to Mithra, from Persian mythology. Mithra was an all-seeing god and whilst wise and benevolent, he was also the war-god and Verethraghna was one of his most potent weapons of revenge: 'sharp in tusk, unapproachable, a raging beast... He smashes the backbone. At one fell blow he destroys everything: bones and hair, brains and blood of men who break their contracts he mashes up together with mud.'

Wonderful Pig of the Ocean Another heraldic beast in the form of a pig with dragon's feet, horns with eyes each side and another eye in its belly, a fish tail and a quarter circle behind its head.

Yale or Yali From southern India, this is really the evolutionary development of the Eale, being a spotted horse with an elephant's tail, boar's tusks and another set of movable horns.

Ysgithyrwyn Another huge wild boar, from Welsh Arthurian legends. This one provided the tusk so that the giant Ysbaddaden could shave for his daughter Olwen's wedding.

HOG THE HERO 6

Pigs Might Fly

Our next hero was around before the Great War, and thus early in the history of flight disproved the old saying about pigs being unable to fly. It was 4 November 1909 and Lord Brabazon of Tara was the first holder of a pilot's licence in Britain. (His cars always carried his personal registration number, FLY1.) He attached a receptacle to his Short biplane into which a young piglet was placed with a placard reading 'I am the first pig to fly' before taking it on a brief flight of around three-and-a-half miles or so.

A British Saddleback sow.

HOG THE HERO 7

Fire

In a suburb of Chicago, a sow was observed to save her newborn piglets by carrying them, one at a time, from a burning barn, just like a cat carries her young. The sow brought out piglets one, two and three and returned a fourth time into the blazing building but was not seen again.

SOW STATUESQUE!

The gates to Charlcote Park, a National Trust property in Warwick-shire, are watched over by two magnificent stone heraldic boars.

The entrance to Charlcote Park.

NAME YOUR PIG

Baconer – a pig of 83–101kgs live-weight, suitable for the production of bacon

Barrow – a male pig castrated young for meat production (US)

Boar – an uncastrated male pig of sexual maturity (also applied to the male of the badger, bear and weasel species)

Brawn – an old name for a young boar

Brawner – a boar castrated after having been used for service

Brimming – a term applied to a female pig during her heat

Butcher pig – a pig ready to kill, at 100kgs live-weight (US)

Cut sow – a spayed female, once common for fattening

Cutter – a pig weighing 68-82kgs live-weight

➥

Dam – the mother pig, used in pedigree recording (also grand-dam, etc.)

Doylt – a tame swine

Dryft – a collective noun for a group or herd of domestic pigs, rarely used today

A dryft of swine as illustrated on an old postcard.

Farrow – to give birth (from Old English *fearh* meaning a young pig)

Feeder pig – American term for a store pig between weaning and slaughter

Gilt – a young female up to the rearing of her first litter (dialect variations include: barrow, elt, gelt, helt, hilt, yelt, yilt)

Herd – the collective noun for a group of domesticated pigs

Hog – a castrated male pig raised for meat (also in the US the more general term for a pig, usually having reached 100lbs in weight)

In-pig – pregnant ('lined' is an obsolete term for this)

Litter – the group of piglets from a single birth up to the point of weaning

Market pig – same as butcher pig above

➡

Piglet/pigling – the newly born pigs in a litter up to the point of weaning

Porker – a pig weighing 50–67kgs live-weight

Rig – a boar with only one testicle visible

Runner – American term for a store pig, i.e. between a weaner and a porker

Runt – the smallest pig in the litter (dialect variations include: bonham, bonneen, bonnine, cad, cadma, cadman, creek, crink, crut, dag, darling, dawlin, derlin, dilling, dillon, doll, dolling, dorling, harry-pig, nesslegraf, nestle-tripe, niscal, nisgo, nisgull, niskral, nistledriff, parson's pig, piggywhidden, pitman, ratlin, ratling, reckling, rickling, rit, ritling, shargar, squeaker, tantony pig, waster, water-droger, wossett, wreckling, wreg)

Originally named after Runtington Farm nearby, the sign now depicts a small pig (the runt) in a barrel. Maynards Green, near Heathfield, East Sussex.

Service – the act of mating

Shoat – a newly weaned pig

Shot – a pig of 9–12 months old which was considered fit to kill for pork (17th C); by the early 19th century the age of a shot had reduced to 6–8 months but today it would be between just over 4 months and 6 months ➡➜

Sire – the father pig, used in pedigree recording (also grand-sire, etc.)

Sounder – the name given to a group of wild boar

Sow – a female which has produced a litter of pigs

Stag – a male pig castrated late for meat production (US)

Stores – the term for young pigs between weaners and porkers

Swine – a collective name for pigs

Teats – the pig's mammary glands, of which there should be at least 12, evenly spaced, and preferably more (dialect variations: dills, drills)

Tusker – a name applied to an old, solitary wild boar

Udder – the double banked row of teats as a whole (colloquially known in America as the 'milk bottles' or 'dinner baskets')

Weaner – the young pig after weaning (dialect: slip)

Wilgil/wildew – a hermaphrodite pig, having both sets of sex organs but invariably being sterile

THE HOG-FACED GENTLEWOMAN OF WIRKHAM

This story dates back to 1640 when a pamphlet was published about 'Mistris Tannakin Skinker' from Wirkham in the Netherlands, born in 1618. As a result of a witch's curse on her mother for refusing her begging plea for money, 'As the Mother is Hoggish, so Swinish shall be the Child', the child was born with a pig's snout. The original text ran: '… all the limbes and lineaments of her body well featur'd and proportion'd, only her face, which is the ornament and beauty of the rest, had the Nose of a Hog, or Swine, which was not only a stain and blemish, but a deformed

➤

uglinesse, making all the rest loathsome, contemptible and odious to all that look upon her...'

A magician, Vandermast, was consulted and he advised that the curse would be broken if a suitable suitor could be found to marry the girl. Extensive efforts were made including the offering of a dowry of £40,000 and even introducing her to potential suitors with her head covered by a black bag. One Scotsman is said to have escaped, as '... he could endure no Porke' .

No willing gentleman was found and it is believed that the unfortunate Mistress Skinker lived out her days in luxury in London.

> Hee will sonnet a whole quire of paper in praise of Lady Swin-snout, his yeolow-fac's Mistres.'
>
> – Thomas Nashe [*Pierce Penilesse, his supplication to the Divell*]

THE PIG-FACED
LADY OF MANCHESTER SQUARE

Nearly 200 years later, in 1815, a broadsheet was published by H. Humphrey of St James's Street. 'This extraordinary female is about 18 years of age, of High rank and great fortune. Her body and limbs are of the most perfect and beautiful shape but her head and face resembles that of a Pig. She eats her victuals out of a Silver Trough in the same manner as Pigs do and when spoken to she can only answer by Grunting; her chief amusement is the Piano on which she plays most delightfully.'

It was claimed that a young baronet, Sir William Elliot, on calling at the address: '... found a person fashionably dressed, who, on turning towards him, displayed a hideous pig's face. Sir William, a timid young gentleman, could not refrain from uttering a shout of horror, and rushed to the door in a manner the reverse of polite; then the infuriated lady or animal, uttering a series of grunts, rushed at the unfortunate baronet as he was retreating, and inflicted a severe wound on the back of his neck...'

She could not keep servants and an advertisement for a maid appeared in *The Times* in February 1815 and subsequently, a week later, an advertisement was placed in the *Morning Herald* by a gentleman wishing for a

➤

formal introduction. However, the story fizzled out when it transpired that it was being mirrored by a similar account of another such female residing in Dublin.

Both these stories may have been inspired by the story of King Oisin of Tir na nÓg in Celtic mythology.

There was one other notable person who had pig-like features. Known in his youth as Bucca Porci (Peter Pig's Snout), his contemporaries continued to refer to him thus even after he had become Pope Sergius IV (1009-1012). No respect, even then!

Today, 'Pig's Snout' or 'Proboscis' is a recognised medical condition, being a deformity in which the two sides of the nose fail to fuse, and is entirely treatable by plastic surgery.

THE WONDERFUL MISS ATKINSON.
Born in Ireland has £ 20000 fortune and is fed out of a Silver Trough.
GEORGE MORLAND.
This account is verbatim from the handwriting of the late George Morland on

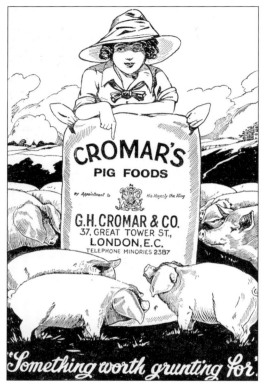

Advertisement for pig feed from 1924.

The Oxford Sandy and Black, a modern breed.

SOW INSULTING!

In 2005, Rolf Harris on his Portrait of the Queen

Harris, 75, said: 'It was a bit stressful when I couldn't get the likeness right. The first rough one was exactly that, just a rough idea. It sort of looked like a pork butcher from Norwich; it didn't look anything like the Queen at all.'

An old tiled sign outside a butcher's shop in Cirencester, Gloucestershire.

From a Letter to *The Daily Telegraph*, September 1996

Sir – On the subject of whether or not to pop champagne corks, a friend was dining at a London restaurant, her escort being a regular client well known to the staff. Champagne was ordered and, as it happened, a couple at a nearby table also ordered a bottle. It was opened by a waiter with a loud pop, hailed with cries of 'Bravo!'. At my friend's table, however, the bottle was opened slowly, with barely an audible hiss.

She asked the waiter: 'Why didn't our bottle go off with a bang, like the one over there?' The waiter, bending down, whispered: 'Madam, the gentleman at that table is a pork butcher, they expect it.'

– John Bunting, Godalming, Surrey

Piggy Quotations

In Sympathy

Glad I'm not a pig.
– HRH Prince Charles, The Prince of Wales (Newspaper report, May 1978, of a visit to an intensive pig unit at Stoneleigh)

———

The pig, if I am not mistaken,
Supplies us sausage, ham, and bacon.
Let others say his heart is big –
I call it stupid of the pig.
– Ogden Nash, *The Pig*

———

One disadvantage of being a hog is that at any moment some blundering fool may try to make a silk purse out of your wife's ear.
– J.B.Morton (*Beachcomber*) [By The Way, September, Tail-Piece]

A Word from our Fans

Pigs are… troublesome, noysome, unruly, and great ravenours…
– Gervaise Markham, *Cheape and Good Husbandry* (1660)

———

If swine enter a house and scatter about the fire, so as to set the house on fire, and the swine escape, let the owner of the swine pay for the act. If the swine be burnt, then both house and swine are equal, for both are stupid; therefore as both have suffered according to the law, there is nothing to be redressed, but the injury of the one must be set against the injury of the other.
– From the '*Howel Dha*', ancient Welsh laws.

———

'Don't you go getting yourself dirty now!'

The plaguy pigs are never worth the meat,
They neither feed nor are they fit to eat.
– Traditional north-country rhyme extolling the virtues of castration.

Of all the quadrupeds that we know, or at least certainly of all those that come under the husbandman's care, the Hog appears to be the foulest, the most brutish, and the most apt to commit waste wherever it goes. The defects of its figure seem to influence its dispositions: all its ways are gross, all its inclinations are filthy, and all its sensations concentrate in a furious lust, and so eager a gluttony, that it devours indiscriminately whatever comes in its way.
– John Mills, *A Treatise on Cattle* (1776)

I learned long ago never to wrestle with a pig. You get dirty, and besides, the pig likes it.
– George Bernard Shaw

Well-being and happiness never appeared to me as an absolute aim. I am even inclined to compare such moral aims to the ambitions of a pig.
– Albert Einstein [Quoted in C.P. Snow's *Variety of Men*, 1969]

———

The pig can hardly be regarded as a classic animal.
– Donald G. Mitchell, *Rural Studies* (1867)

In Classical Mode

Beside, 'tis known he could speak Greek
As naturally as pigs squeak:
That Latin was no more difficile
Than to a blackbird 'tis to whistle.
– Samuel Butler, *Hudibras*, part 1

———

Think to yourself that every day is your last; the hour to which you do not look forward will come as a welcome surprise. As for me, when you want a good laugh, you will find me, in a fine state, fat and sleek, a true hog of Epicurus' herd.
– Horace (Quintus Horatius Flaccus) *Epistles, book 1*

———

It is better to be Socrates dissatisfied than a pig satisfied.
– John Stuart Mill, *Utilitarianism*

Reasons to be Greedy

Pig, n. An animal (Porcus omniverous) closely allied to the human race by the splendour and vivacity of its appetite, which, however, is inferior in scope, for it sticks at pig.

– Ambrose Bierce, *The Devil's Dictionary* (1881)

The two biggest little pigs have been sold, which takes away from the completeness of the family group… But their appetites were fearful – five meals a day and not satisfied. The pigs are mostly sold, at what drapers call a 'sacrifice'. They seem to me to have devoured most of my potatoes before their departure. I was extremely amused during my drive in the trap; Cannon kept pointing out cottages – 'Do you see that house? They've bought one pig! Do you see yon? They've bought two pigs!' The whole district is planted out with my pigs; but we still take an interest in them because if they grow well we shall 'get a name for pigs'. Such is fame!

– Beatrix Potter, quoted in *The Tale of Beatrix Potter* by Margaret Lane (1968)

The Berkshire was the breed kept by Beatrix Potter, something she had in common with Queen Victoria.

Playing with Words

The boar-pig had drawn nearer to the gate for a closer inspection of the human intruders, and stood clamping his jaws and blinking his small red eyes in a manner that was doubtless intended to be disconcerting, and, as far as the Stossens were concerned, thoroughly achieved that result.

'Shoo! Hish! Hish! Shoo!' cried the ladies in chorus.

'If they think they're going to drive him away by reciting lists of the Kings of Israel and Judah they're laying themselves out for disappointment,' observed Matilda...
– Saki, *The Boar-Pig* (1914)

This is not a thing which, as the proverb says, 'any pig would know'.
– Plato, *Laches* (*c*. 375 BC)

He took me down to see the pigs... and we talked pigs all the way.
– A. A. Milne, *Mr Pim Passes By* (1922)

The Practical

LAUNCELOT: ...this making of Christians will raise the price of hogs: if we grow all to be pork-eaters, we shall not shortly have a rasher on the coals for money.
– William Shakespeare, *The Merchant of Venice*, Act III, sc.5

Horse-high, pig-tight and bull-strong.
– Definition of a legal boundary fence in America

I don't know whether to kill you and eat you or sell you and drink you.
– Anonymous Irish farmer addressing his pig

On Imbibing

One evening in October,
When I was far from sober,
And dragging home a load with manly pride,
My feet began to stutter,
So I laid down in the gutter,
And a pig came up and parked right by my side.
Then I warbled, 'It's fair weather
When good fellows get together,'
Til a lady passing by was heard to say:

'You can tell a man who boozes
By the company he chooses.'
Then the pig got up and slowly walked away.
– Benjamin Hapgood Burt (Song written in 1933)

⟡

They lay and slept like drunken swine.
– John Lydgate, *Fall of Princes* (c. 1480)

A Contrary View

Pigs grunt in a wet wallow-bath, and smile as they snort and dream. They dream of the acorned swill of the world, the rooting for pigfruit, the bag-pipe dugs of the mother sow, the squeal and snuffle of yesses of the women pigs in rut. They mud-bask and snout in the pig-loving sun; their tails curl; they rollick and slobber and snore to deep, smug, after-swill sleep.
– Dylan Thomas, *Under Milk Wood* (1954)

⟡

The work of teaching and organising the others fell naturally upon the pigs, who were generally recognised as being the cleverest of the animals.
– George Orwell, *Animal Farm* (1945)

Three gruntlings.

Pastoral Scenes

And pigs he rung, and bells he hung,
And horses shod and cured.

– Traditional verse, on the work of the farrier

Already fallen plum-bloom stars the green
And apple-boughs as knarred as old toad's backs
Wear their small roses ere a rose is seen;
The building thrush watches old Job who stacks
The bright-peeled osiers on the sunny fence,
The pent sow grunts to hear him stumping by,
And tries to push the bolt and scamper thence,
But her ringed snout still keeps her to the sty.

Then out he lets her run; away she snorts
In bundling gallop for the cottage door,
With hungry hubbub begging crusts and orts,
Then like a whirlwind bumping round once more;
Nuzzling the dog, making the pullets run,
And sulky as a child when her play's done.

– Edmund Blunden (1896–1974), *The Poor Man's Pig*

Considering the End Product (1)

A couple of flitches of bacon are worth fifty thousand Methodist sermons and religious tracts… They are great softeners of the temper and promoters of domestic harmony.'

– William Cobbett

I've lived on swine 'til I grunt and squeal,
No one can tell how my bowels feel,
With slapjacks swimming in bacon grease,
I'm a lousy miner,
I'm a lousy miner, when will my troubles cease?
– Verse from a song from the Californian gold rush of the 1850s

He who cannot eat horsemeat need not do so. Let him eat pork. But he who cannot eat pork, let him eat horsemeat. It's simply a question of taste.
– Nikita Khruschev, former premier of the USSR

This pig, which was eaten many times in anticipation, had at length fallen victim to the butcher, and Facey's larder was uncommonly well found in black-puddings, sausages, spareribs, and the other component parts of a pig; so that he was in very hospitable circumstances – at least, in his rough and ready idea of what hospitality ought to be. Indeed, whether he had or not, he'd have risked it, being quite as good at carrying things off with a high hand as Mr Sponge himself.
– Surtees (Robert Smith Surtees) (1805–1864), *Mr Sponge's Sporting Tour*

The quality and variety of produce from the humble pig has always been well appreciated.

Slightly Bizarre

'You don't happen to know why they killed the pig, do you?' retorts Mr Bucket…'Why, they killed him… on account of his having so much cheek.'
– Charles Dickens, *Bleak House*

———⌇⌇⌇———

But the wild exultation was suddenly checked,
When the jailer informed them, with tears,
Such a sentence could not have the slightest effect,
As the pig had been dead for some years.
– Lewis Carroll (The Reverend Charles Lutwidge Dodgson), *The Hunting Of The Snark*

———⌇⌇⌇———

Down the river did glide, with wind and with tide,
A pig with vast celerity;
And the Devil looked wise as he saw how the while
It cut its own throat. 'There!' quoth he, with a smile,
'Goes England's commercial prosperity.'
– Samuel Taylor Coleridge, *The Devil's Thoughts*

———⌇⌇⌇———

As a jewel of gold in a swine's snout, so is a fair woman which is without discretion.
– The Bible, *Proverbs*, ch. ii, v. 22

———⌇⌇⌇———

The pill of life needs sweetening. There will, inevitably, be instances of that sweetening seeming absurd, like a pig parading in a tutu.
– Petronella Wyatt, *The Sunday Telegraph* (May 1995)

———⌇⌇⌇———

There was an old person of Ealing,
Who was wholly devoid of good feeling;
He drove a small gig,
With three Owls and a Pig,
Which distressed all the people of Ealing.
– Edward Lear, *One Hundred Nonsense Pictures and Rhymes*

———⌇⌇⌇———

A Touch of Greed

Every little helps, as the sow said, when she snapped at a gnat.

– C. H. Spurgeon, *John Ploughman*

—◁⟨⟨⟩⟩▷—

Bulls make money, Bears make money,
But greedy pigs never do.

– London Stock Market saying

—◁⟨⟨⟩⟩▷—

A gentleman passing through Burslem a few days since, had his attention arrested by the agitation of an oak tree, from whence the acorns fell in showers. On approaching it, he observed eleven young pigs faring on the fruit, whilst the mother-sow which had ascended the tree, clung with her fore-legs to an upper branch, and shook the lower with her left hind leg.

– A report in the *Shrewsbury Chronicle*, 25 October 1811

—◁⟨⟨⟩⟩▷—

Lawsuit, n., a machine which you go into as a pig and come out of as a sausage.

Edible, adj., good to eat, and wholesome to digest, as a worm to a toad, a toad to a snake, a snake to a pig, a pig to a man, and a man to a worm.

– Ambrose Bierce, *The Devil's Dictionary*

—◁⟨⟨⟩⟩▷—

Now, as for dirt, pigs are really very clean creatures if given proper accommodation and some decent straw. As for greed, certainly not even the most sincere apologist of pigs or lover of bacon can deny that they enjoy their victuals. But reflect, reader, how it would be with you if you had an immensely long, barrel-shaped and capacious body carried on four very short legs: if you had a nose (or snout) especially constructed and designed to go to the root of matters: if you had a mouth of peculiar capacity, stretching almost from ear to ear. (And, by the way, what charming ears, too, eminently adapted for flapping and, at the same time, for composing the eye for slumber beneath their ample shade!)

Would you not enjoy your food even more than you do now? Would you not grunt, and even slightly squeal, with an excruciating ecstasy of creamy, rich barley-meal, as it entered your long and wide mouth, gurgled in your roomy throat and flowed on into that vast stomach forever clamouring to be soothed?

– John Beresford (1873–1947), *Storm and Peace*

A Little Religion

Give not that which is holy unto the dogs, neither cast ye your pearls before swine, lest they trample them under their feet, and turn again and rend you.

– The Bible, *Matthew*, ch. vii, v. 6

There warn't anybody at the church, except maybe a hog or two, for there warn't any lock on the door, and hogs likes a puncheon floor in summertime because it's cool. If you notice, most folks don't go to church only when they've got to; but a hog is different.

– Mark Twain (Samuel Langhorne Clemens), *The Adventures of Huckleberry Finn*

The Parsons Pig, Pound Hill, near Horsham in West Sussex.

Dear Mr Lansbury stands for our happy exposure to perfect annihilation. With broad amiability he is ready any day for the Gadarene gallop on the back of his own whole hog.

– J. L. Garvin, *The Observer* (1937)

—◦◦◦—

'Of course,' said the leader of the Gadarene swine,
Rushing furiously towards the sea,
'One knows
That the rest don't really want
To come over this steep place
But what can one do?
I often wonder,' he went on, panting,
'How we were manoeuvred
Into this position!'

– Richard Mallett, Translations from *The Ish*

—◦◦◦—

'This man', said McTurk, with conviction, 'is the Gadarene Swine'.

– Rudyard Kipling, *The Flag of their Country* from *Stalky & Co*

Just one of many pigs depicted in churches in the UK. This carving on a misericord at Bristol Cathedral shows a man on a sow jousting with a woman on a goose.

CELEBRATING
THE PIG – LA POURCAILHADE

In rural France there is an annual festival to celebrate the pig, which takes place around the middle of August each year. Called '*La pourcailhade*' it is held in Trie sur Baise in the Hautes-Pyrenees and includes a number of jolly pig-related activities including a black pudding eating competition, a fancy dress competition and pig racing.

There is also a pig-mimicry contest which is divided into categories, such as matching the noises made by the newborn piglet, the pig during castration, the mating sounds, and so on.

The festival includes merry-making of all kinds and is organised by *La Confrérie du Cochon* – The Brotherhood of the Pig.

THE FISHING PIGS OF TONGA

Pigs were introduced on to the Pacific Island of Tonga by the explorer Captain Cook, so as to ensure supplies of fresh meat for future visitors. Their descendants still live there as feral swine and have developed a taste for seafood.

It is now a tourist attraction to see the pigs arriving at low tide to search for tasty morsels of fish, crustaceans and seaweed. The smallest piglets remain in rock pools left by the retreating sea whereas the larger hogs wade out into the water up to their middles, in search of the tastier bits. Fully-grown sows go out as far as the reef. Whilst the pigs don't actually appear to swim, they have adapted their breathing sufficiently to allow them to plunge their heads under the waves for several minutes at a time while hunting.

The resulting pork is much prized by the Islanders and is said to be saltier and more flavoursome than meat from pigs fed a more conventional diet.

I was very disturbed when Jesus found a demon in a guy and He put the demon into a herd of pigs, then sent them off a cliff. What did the pigs do? I could never figure that out. It just seemed very un-Christian.

– Matt Groening, creator of *The Simpsons*

Thus says the prophet of the Turk:
Good mussulman, abstain from pork;
There is a part in ev'ry swine
No friend or follower of mine
May taste, whate'er his inclination,
On pain of excommunication… .
But for one piece they thought it hard
From the whole hog to be debarr'd… .
With sophistry their sauce they sweeten,
Till quite from tail to snout 'tis eaten.

– William Cowper, *The Love of the World Reproved, or Hypocrisy Detected* (1779)

I'm not really a Jew, just Jew-ish, not the whole hog.

– Jonathan Miller

Cleanliness is Next to Godliness

And the swine, though he divide the hoof, and be cloven-footed, yet he cheweth not the cud; he is unclean to you.

– The Bible, *Leviticus*, ch. ii, v. 7–8

It is not swinish to be happy unless one is happy in swinish ways.

– L. Susan Stebbing *Ideals and Illusions*

… pigs and children bask and roll about, and often resemble one another so much, that it is necessary to look twice before the human face divine is confessed. I believe there are more pigs in Mitchelstown than human beings…

– Arthur Young, on Ireland in the late 1770s

Above all things, keep clean. It is not necessary to be a pig in order to raise one.

– R.G. Ingersoll, *About Farming in Illinois* (1877)

⟞⟋⟍⟋⟍⟞

The fatter the sow, the more she desires the mire.

– John Bunyan, *Pilgrim's Progress* (1678)

⟞⟋⟍⟋⟍⟞

We were living in trees when they met us. They showed us each in turn
That Water would certainly wet us, as Fire would certainly burn:
But we found them lacking in Uplift, Vision and Breadth of Mind,
So we left them to teach the Gorillas while we followed the March of
    Mankind…
As it will be in the future, it was at the birth of Man –
There are only four things certain since Social Progress began:
That the Dog returns to his Vomit and the Sow returns to her mire,
And the burnt Fool's bandaged finger goes wobbling back to the fire…

– Rudyard Kipling, *The Gods of the Copybook Headings* (1919)

⟞⟋⟍⟋⟍⟞

What! Ye who grub
With filthy snouts my red potatoes up
In Allan's rushy bog? Who eat the oats
Up, from my cavalry in the Hebrides?
Who swill the hog-wash soup my cooks digest
From bones, and rags, and scraps of shoe-leather,
Which should be given to cleaner pigs than you?

– Percy Bysshe Shelley, *Oedipus Tyrannus or Swellfoot the Tyrant* (1820)

Political Wisdom

It's like embracing a pig.

– President Ronald Reagan (1982 press briefing on the need to raise taxes)

———

Trying to cut red tape is like wrestling with a greasy pig.

– Prime Minister John Major in 1995

How Insulting

You look like a pig, but I suppose we can use you.

– Brian Duffy, photographer (Said to Joanna Lumley on her first modelling assignment)

———

As Romeo he (Irving) reminds me of a pig who has been taught to play the fiddle. He does it cleverly but he would be better employed in squealing.

– Anon (quoted in *The Story of My Life* by Ellen Terry)

———

I have eyes like those of a dead pig.

– Marlon Brando

———

They had him thrown out of a club in Bombay
For, apart from his Mess-bills exceeding his pay,
He took to pig-sticking in quite the wrong way.
I wonder what happened to him!

– Noël Coward, *Sigh No More* (1945)

————

You dirty rotten swine you!

– Bluebottle (Peter Sellers) in *The Goon Show*, BBC Home Service

Considering the End Product (2)

Heigho! My dinner, oh!
Bacon and potatoes, oh!

– A 19th century Wiltshire ditty

————

Lean bacon is the most wasteful thing that a family can use. In short, it is uneatable except by drunkards who want something to stimulate their sickly appetites. The man who cannot live on solid, fat bacon, well fed and well cured, wants the sweet sauce of labour or is fit for the hospital.

– William Cobbett, *Cottage Economy* (1828)

————

I prefer the grunting of a hog in a cottager's sty to the song of the nightingale; and I think sides of bacon the very best furniture of a labourer's cottage.

– An unnamed Dorset squire addressing an agricultural dinner in 1857

————

Clean or Dirty?

There is nothing a pig loves more than a good bath, with a loofah and plenty of soap flakes… There is something delightfully loveable about a really clean pig, in clean yellow straw.

– Barbara Woodhouse, *Talking To Animals* (1954)

The traditional view of the pig is that it is dirty and greedy: The Common Boar is, of all other domestic quadrupeds, the most filthy and impure. Its form is clumsy and disgusting and its appearance gluttonous and excessive.

– Thomas Bewick (1753–1828)

An impromptu bath as this Gloucestershire Old Spots gets in the water trough to cool down.

Wine and Swine

Hog-whimpering drunk.

– Rupert Soames (Industrialist grandson of Sir Winston Churchill)

Upon the first goblet he read this inscription, 'monkey wine'; upon the second, 'lion wine'; upon the third, 'sheep wine'; upon the fourth, 'swine wine'. These four inscriptions expressed the four descending degrees of drunkenness: the first, that which enlivens; the second, that which irritates; the third, that which stupefies; finally the last, that which brutalises.

– Victor Hugo, *Les Miserables* (1862)

April 15th, 1778. Brewed a vessel of strong Beer today. My two large Piggs... got so amazingly drunk by it, that they were not able to stand and appeared like dead things almost, and so remained all night from dinner-time today. I never saw Piggs so drunk in my life. I slit their ears for them without feeling.

April 16th, 1778. My 2 Piggs are still unable to walk yet, but they are better than they were yesterday. They tumble about the yard and can by no means stand at all steady yet. In the evening my 2 Piggs were tolerably sober.

– James Woodforde, *Diary of a Country Parson*

'PIG' IN VARIOUS FOREIGN LANGUAGES

Afrikaans – **vark**
Assyrian – **khzooyrraa**
Basque – **txerri**
Bengali – **shuor**
Breton – **moc'h**
Bulgarian – **svinia**
Chinese – **zhu**
Croatian – **svinja**
Czech – **vepr/svin**
Danish – **gris/svin**
Dutch – **varken/zwijn**
Esperanto – **porco**
Estonian – **siga**
Finnish – **karkko/sika**
French – **cochon/porc**
German – **schwein**
Greek – **delphax/choiros**
Hawaiian – **pua'a**
Hindi – **soor**
Hungarian – **malac/sertes**
Icelandic – **svin**
Indonesian – **babi**
Irish – **muic**

Italian – **maiale/porco**
Japanese – **buta**
Latin – **porca/sus**
Latvian – **cuka**
Lithuanian – **kiaule**
Maltese – **qazquz**
Manx – **banbh**
Maori – **poaka**
Norwegian – **gris**
Polish – **prosiak/swinia**
Portuguese – **leito/porco**
Punjabi – **soor**
Romanian – **porc**
Russian – **svynya**
Serbo-Croatian – **syinja**
Shetlandic – **grice**
Spanish – **cerdo/puerco**
Swahili – **nguruwe**
Swedish – **gris/svin**
Turkish – **domuz**
Urdu – **soo'ar**
Vietnamese – **con lo n**

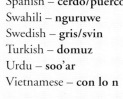

The British Lop is Britain's rarest pig breed. It originated on the Devon and Cornwall borders.

Gourmands Unite

In his (or her) lifetime the average Briton eats 8 cattle, 36 sheep, 36 pigs, and 550 poultry. Imagine seeing this sizeable herd in a field – and being told that you would have to eat your way through them!

– David Jacobs, Article in *RSPCA Today* (1983)

———

Pig. This is the king of unclean beasts; whose empire is most universal, whose qualities are least in question: no pig, no lard, and consequently, no cooking, no ham, no sausages, no andouilles, no black puddings and finally no pork-butchers. Ungrateful doctors! You have condemned the pig: he is, as regards indigestion, one of the finest feathers in your cap.

– Grimod de la Reynière, *Calendrier Gastronomique* (*c.* 1800)

———

Nothing helps scenery like bacon and eggs.

– Mark Twain, *Roughing It*

———

The pig, by a merciful providence, was given to mankind solely for our benefit and in order to supplement our diet.

– Olaus Magnus (1490–1557)

THE SOUNDS PIGS MAKE ACROSS THE WORLD

Afrikaans – **oink-oink**	Hungarian – **rof-rof-rof**
Albanian – **hunk hunk**	Japanese – **buubuu**
Catalan – **onk-onk**	Korean – **kkool-kkool**
Chinese – **hu-lu hu-lu**	Norwegian – **noff-noff**
Croatian – **rok-rok**	Polish – **chrum chrum**
Danish – **of**	Portuguese – **oink-oink**
Dutch – **varkens knorren**	Russian – **khryu-khryu**
English – **oink oink**	Spanish – **oink-oink**
Estonian – **rui rui**	Swedish – **noff**
Finnish – **roh roh**	Thai – **ood ood**
French – **groin groin**	Vietnamese – **ut-it**
German – **Schweine grunzen**	

I'm very fond of pigs, but I don't find it difficult to eat them.
– Lord Runcie, former Archbishop of Canterbury

Pigs – For and Against

The hog can raise a mortgage, give you lard and take care of your garbage –
he's the best there is.
– A hog farmer in Colorado

A peasant becomes fond of his pig and is glad to salt away its pork. What is
significant, and is so difficult for the urban stranger to understand, is that
the two statements are connected by an and, and not by a but.
– John Berger

There have even been those who are allergic to pigs: A learned man told
me… that he knew one at Antwerp, that would immediately swoon, as oft
as a pig was set before him, upon any table where he was present.
– Nathaniel Wanley, *Wonders of the Little World* (1678)

Oh Winged Thing

'The time has come' the Walrus said,
'To talk of many things.
Of shoes – and ships – and sealing wax –
Of cabbages – and kings –
And why the sea is boiling hot –
And whether pigs have wings.'
– Lewis Carroll, *Through the Looking Glass*

The paradise of my fancy is one where pigs have wings.
– G.K.Chesterton, *Fancies Versus Fads* (1923)

PIGS AS WORLD LEADERS

In 1967, Jerry Rubin (1938–1994) campaigned to have a pig elected as President of the USA.

In Britain, ambition is a little more modest. During the late 1990s, Winnie was the name given to a pig penned outside the Houses of Parliament to highlight a protest about low incomes for the country's livestock farmers. Winnie, rather like Babe, was in fact more than one pig. Animal rights protesters bought the original Winnie to 'save' her but the canny livestock farmers immediately replaced her in the obvious hope that they had found the answer to their economic ills.

In 2000, another 'Winnie' came to the fore, being nominated as a candidate for the election for Mayor of London. However, Ken Livingstone was given a clear run when the Returning Officer declared that, according to law, candidates had to be human.

POLITICALLY INCORRECT PIG

A Dorset pig farmer made the headlines in 1993 when a complaint was made to the Southampton Racial Equality Council about his Large Black sow, which he had called *Oprah* after the television chat show hostess. After being told that 'this promotes the image that black people are pigs' he offered to change the name to something else.

A Champion Large Black sow from 1907.

Pigs in Politics

They'd vote for a pig as long as it had a red rosette on round here…
Ken Livingstone, then MP for Brent East, during the General Election campaign.
– *The Daily Telegraph*, 25 April 1997

No man should be allowed to be president who does not understand hogs.
– President Harry S. Truman

———

There is no such thing as a perfect leader either in the past or present, in China or elsewhere. If there is one, he is only pretending, like a pig inserting scallions into its nose in an effort to look like an elephant.
– Liu Shao-ch'i, Chinese leader (1898–1969)

———

A pig won't believe anything he can't see.
– Abraham Lincoln

———

We are being asked to buy a pig in a poke. It is always the same pig and always the same poke and it has never yet been delivered.
– Lord Tebbit on the Northern Ireland peace process, July 1999

Playing with Words

… like he has a ring on his nose – like a pig going to market.
Emma Nicholson on the influence of the Eurosceptic Tories over John Major, which she claimed was the reason for her defection to the Liberal Democrats.
– *The Sunday Telegraph*, January 1996

———

The pig has lived only to eat, he eats only to die… He eats everything his gluttonous snout touches, he will be eaten completely… he eats all the time, he will be eaten all the time… The pig is nothing but an enormous dish which walks while waiting to be served… In a sort of photograph of future destiny, everything announces that he will be eaten, but eaten in such a fashion that there will remain of him not the smallest bone, not a hair, not an atom.

– Charles Monselet, *Lettres Gourmandes* (1874)

In the argot of the cycle world, a Harley is a 'hog' and the outlaw bike is a 'chopped hog'. Basically, it is the same machine all motorcycle cops use, but the police bike is an accessory-loaded elephant compared to the lean, customised dynamos the Hell's Angels ride. The resemblance is about the same as that of a factory-equipped Cadillac to a dragster's stripped-down essence of the same car.

– Hunter S. Thompson, *Hell's Angels* (1966)

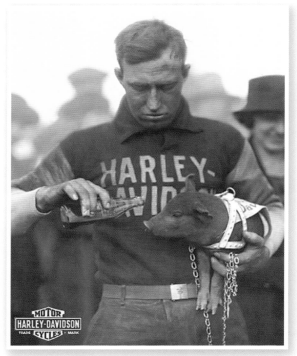

Refuelling the hog.

Being Upstaged

Nobody cared if I'd powdered my nose. When the pig was ready, we began shooting. In a sense it was most humiliating to share billing with a pig, but who wants to fight success?

– Eva Gabor, on working with 'Arnold Ziffel', the show-stealing pig on *Green Acres*, a television show of the 1960s

And finally…

Pigs are pigs.

– Charles Lamb in a letter to Samuel Taylor Coleridge in 1822